SIGNS OF THE TIMES

Some Recurring Motifs in Twentieth-Century Photography

10 May—14 July 1985

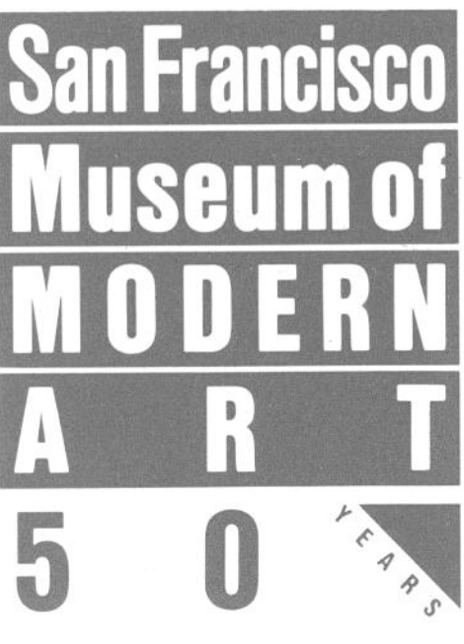

Library of Congress
Cataloging in Publication Data
San Francisco Museum of Modern Art.
Signs of the Times.

1. Photography, Artistic—Exhibitions. I. Irmas,
Deborah, 1950-   . II. Title.
TR646.U6S369 1985   799'.09'04074019461   85-2280

ISBN: 0-918471-01-X

The Museum is supported in part by the Institute of
Museum Services, the National Endowment for the Arts,
the San Francisco Hotel Tax Fund, and the San Francisco
Foundation.

Design: Suzanne Anderson-Carey
Photography: Ben Blackwell
Typesetting: petrographics/typeworld
Printing: Tom Larkey Creative Printing

Cover:
LOTTI JACOBI
69. *Head of a Dancer, Berlin,*
1929/bet. 1978-79 (detail)

SIGNS OF THE TIMES

Some Recurring Motifs in Twentieth-Century Photography

Contents

Acknowledgements ... 4

Foreword by Van Deren Coke ... 5

Signs of the Times: Some Recurring Motifs in Twentieth-Century Photography
by Deborah Irmas ... 6

Plates ... 22

Checklist of the Exhibition ... 50

Board of Trustees and Staff ... 56

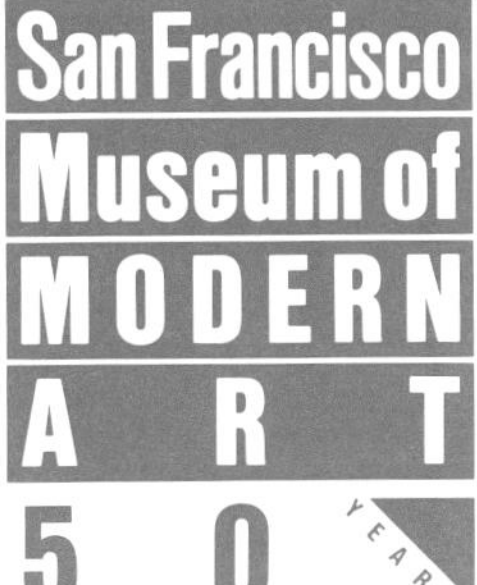

Acknowledgements

Van Deren Coke's invitation in the spring of 1983 to look at the permanent collection of photography shelf by shelf, photograph by photograph, was like the realization of the childhood dream of being locked inside a candy shop. Those months of gazing at thousands of images without the constraints of a predetermined study produced two projects: *The Implied Performance,* an exhibition of contemporary photography created especially for California State University at Northridge in March 1984; and *Signs of the Times: Some Recurring Motifs in Twentieth-Century Photography,* one of many exhibitions celebrating the fiftieth anniversary of the San Francisco Museum of Modern Art. In both instances, Van Deren Coke encouraged me to consider the collection from unusual vantage points, good-naturedly allowing me to exercise my penchant for pitting formidable icons of the medium next to less significant photographic artifacts in my effort to reveal some notion of a collective vision. If my approach or reasoning proves specious, it should reflect neither upon the Director of Photography nor the Museum. If, however, any contribution is made here, it is the direct result of Van Deren Coke's generosity with his vast knowledge, experience, and ideas.

Without exception, the entire staff at the San Francisco Museum of Modern Art was warm and gracious to me, and without their help this project could not have been realized. Especially helpful was Diana duPont, Research Assistant II, who, among other duties, oversees research and cataloging of the Museum's permanent collection of photography. With Research Assistant Sara Leith, she steadfastly revised, edited, and translated entries of the checklist so that it conformed with Museum standards. In as much as many of the photographs listed here have never or rarely been exhibited, this proved to be a thankless task. Patti Carroll, Curatorial Assistant, Department of Photography, coordinated the photographs for the exhibition as well as the reproductions for the catalog and proofread the publication material. Karin Victoria, Curatorial Secretary, Department of Photography, refined and shaped the exhibition checklist into its final form, and also assisted in proofreading the publication material. Marcy Reed, Secretary, Research/Collections, ably oversaw the data processing of the checklist. The editorial skills of Lynne Creighton Neall and Anne Munroe, Exhibitions and Publications Coordinator, and Graphic Designer Suzanne Anderson's talent have turned raw manuscript pages into an elegant document of the exhibition.

Friends encouraged me with their help, enthusiasm, and insights including Jonathan Taylor, Jim Hugunin, Patty Detroit, Jo Ann Callis, and Judy Fiskin. My mother and father, Audrey and Sydney Irmas, as always, are my closest allies and supporters of my creative pursuits.

D.I.

Foreword

In the spring of 1983, Deborah Irmas was appointed for a three-month period to the curatorial staff of the Department of Photography to carry out a specific project. She was given the assignment of studying the Museum's entire photography collection and developing fresh ways to combine prints so as to throw new light on the history of the medium in the twentieth century. Drawing on her training in art history and experience teaching the history of photography at the University of Southern California in Los Angeles, she began to sort out motifs that became popular as symbols of new attitudes in this period, then, as they became familiar, metamorphosed into new symbols as times and photographers changed. Due to the relationships she discovered, we see patterns that developed as new subjects captured the imagination of creative photographers seeking to reach a new audience. Her effort is not intended as a finished treatment of her theme; rather it is more a preliminary sketch to set off historians and critics on a new tack. She has persuasively answered many questions about the meaning these subjects have and offered explanations about the attraction of motifs inherited from previous generations, as well as those used for the first time in our century.

She shows us, for example, how a motif such as feet or female legs can take on varied implications. There is a big jump from the legs of a chic model used by Yva for a sensuous display of hose to the legs of a doll used in a carefully assembled organization of disparate elements with strange sexual connotations, photographed by Frederick Sommer. The Yva photograph is teasing, immediate, and perhaps meant to refer to the most famous legs in Yva's Berlin: those of Marlene Dietrich. Sommer's legs are dreamy and mysterious and speak of the soul of art—the evocation of a sense of disturbing ambiguity with deep psychological connotations. Irmas makes the jump gracefully and gives us an indication of the processes of thinking that have gone on in the twentieth century as photographers have explored new ways to grip our imagination for the short- and long-term.

Scholars studying the ancient civilization of Athens and the admirers of that period in history only need fragments of buildings or broken pieces of sculpture or of ceramic vessels to feel the great achievements of classical Greece. Advertising and fine art photographers, using a modern version of this idea, probably taken as much from films as from art museums, moved in close to subjects to convey a sense of mystery, as in Roger Parry's picture of a hand by a gun, or to concentrate the attention of a potential buyer on the attractiveness of stockings worn by a pair of beautiful, anonymous legs. The photographer, by restricting the picture to just legs, encouraged the consumer in her mind's eye to see herself wearing those same stockings. In other words, the close-up of a fragment was all that was needed to sell members of the newly affluent society the stream of products that flowed from the application of new technologies. Paul Strand made, for slightly different reasons, detailed pictures such as those of the interior mechanism of his Akeley movie camera. His beautifully detailed photographs celebrated in the 1920s the ability of manufacturers to make millimetrically precise parts for all kinds of large and small machines and thereby to benefit society. Anton Bruehl applied the same idea in his 1927 picture, made for commercial purposes, of a close-up of giant lightbulbs. This is just one of a number of instances in which Irmas helps us realize that photographers working on assignment applied the lessons of those few photographers in the 1920s who were making pictures for purely philosophic and artistic purposes.

On the one hand, the photographers used the close-up to follow contemporary artists into abstraction, and, on the other hand, details became a new shorthand visual language used to express the increasingly fast pace and fragmentation of life that has characterized our century. The photographer provided a sign, or signaled a clue, and the rest of the information was filled in as we became adept at reading fragments seen out of the windows of rapidly moving cars, buses, and airplanes.

Irmas has added another dimension to the pleasure of just looking at photographs. The usual external way of regarding photographs, that is, mere recognition of the subject before the camera, has been challenged. In doing so she has not neglected style or context in the discussion of her views. Her conclusions broaden our appreciation of factors in twentieth-century photography that are significant from esthetic as well as historic standpoints.

Van Deren Coke
Director
Department of Photography

SIGNS OF THE TIMES

Some Recurring Motifs in Twentieth-Century Photography by Deborah Irmas

While we believe ourselves to identify…motifs on the basis of our practical experience pure and simple, we really read 'what we see' according to the manner in which objects and events were expressed by forms under varying historical conditions.

Erwin Panofsky

"There's the house!" his mother said as if they were all blind but her. It rose on the crest of a hill—a white two story farm house with a wide porch and pleasant columns."

Flannery O'Connor [1]

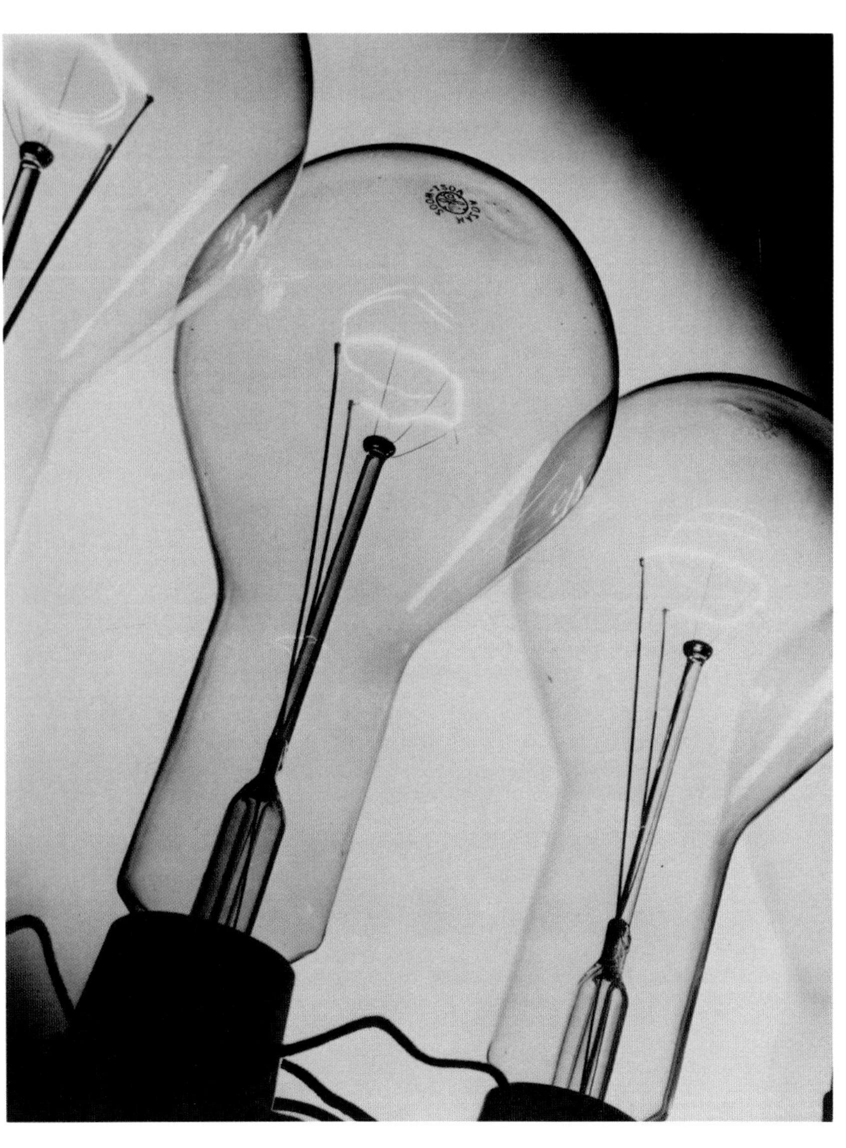

ANTON BRUEHL
4. 6,000 Watts, 1927/1978

An exhibition examining more than seventy years of twentieth-century photography from the perspective of recurrent motifs seems somewhat like exclaiming, "There's the house!" Since one of photography's most interesting and problematic properties is its so-called assumption of "the thing itself," the primary response to any photograph is usually to determine what is being photographed. To point out objects, faces, or disembodied parts of the human figure, that reappear continuously in photography, could be an exercise in stating the obvious. Yet, a large enough sample of twentieth-century images—from those that were nourished by Constructivism in the 1920s to those that show de-Constructivist tendencies of more recent vintage—might indeed alter our beliefs about change within the medium. Photographers may have found different solutions for structuring their photographs over the last seven decades, but they have enjoyed, it seems, looking at many of the same things.

The 225 photographs included in this exhibition
fall into one of two categories. Either they picture the
human figure (or parts thereof), or they picture objects
created in this century. Simply stated, this exhibition looks
at how (and how often) we look at ourselves and the
artifacts of our era. Part I follows photography's first
venture into this uncharted territory: those initial con-
tacts with the likes of airplanes, automobiles, and lightbulbs, together with the experimental recordings of the
human figure served into severed Surrealist portions.
Part II follows the endurance of these motifs from the
Second World War to the present day. In this section,
the use and reapportionment of the figure, that
appeared so provocative in the earlier years, becomes
standard syntax in the language of photography by
the 1960s. Conversely, photographic work from 1977
on reexplored many of the man-made objects glorified
by photographers in the 1920s and early 1930s. But
the dispassionate eye of the earlier era aged into a
cynical one. Consider two examples: Anton Bruehl's
cool display of lightbulbs which he exaggerates with
the title *6,000 Watts*, 1927 (cat. 4), becomes, a half
century later, James Hajicek's still life of discarded
flashbulbs and electrical paraphernalia (cat. 220).
Bruehl's contemporaries showed us promises for the
emerging century, our contemporaries reveal the hard
realities.

This search for twentieth-century common
denominators—threads, if you will—tying the disparate
chapters of photography's last seventy years together
into a cohesive story line, is the task undertaken by the
San Francisco Museum of Modern Art. The Museum's
collection of photography has existed since its inception
in 1935, the same year the Museum opened its doors.
Indeed, the diversity, breadth, and international nature
of the collection, as it has more recently evolved under
the direction of Van Deren Coke, allows it to stand as
a microcosm of the medium's performance in the realm
of fine art. From the pictorial work of the Photo-
Secessionists and the European experiments of the
"New Vision" photographers of the 1920s and 1930s,
to the f.64 photographers and their rebellious mixed-
media progeny of the 1970s, the Museum's holdings
include important icons as well as lesser-known works
of art of this century.

How the San Francisco Museum of Modern Art
has built its permanent collection of photography is
a consideration pertinent to this project. The collection
grew not as a larger compilation of smaller private
collections brought together and displayed by the
Museum, but was acquired slowly, photograph by
photograph, or in small groups. A large part of the
Museum's holdings came as gifts. Artists, dealers,
collectors, and patrons donated works of art to build
upon the ever-expanding corpus. The collection, then,
is not a cohesive representation of one or several
persons' particular choices. Instead it is the ongoing
project of a community. A single work of art purchased
by a patron, for example, will most likely reflect the
personal taste of that person while the work is in his
or her possession, but once it is housed in the Museum,
those attributes disappear to all except those who
know of the donor. Since museums are considered

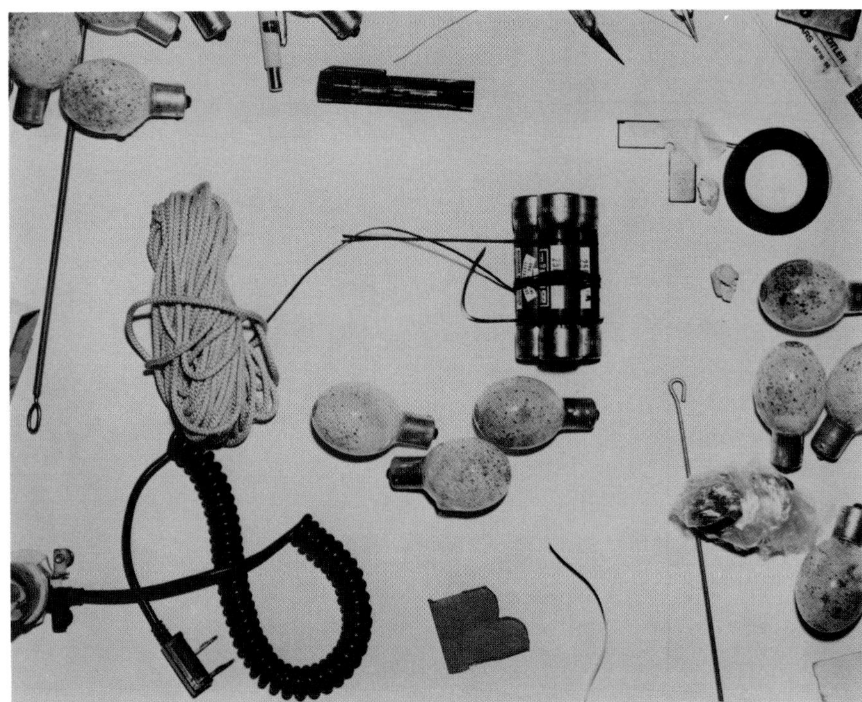

standard-bearers of taste, the piece may acquire a
patina of legitimacy in its new context, but as years
pass and preferences change, the piece is weighed
according to its comparison with greater and lesser
acquisitions that join it. It may be exhibited regularly
or never see the fluorescent light of scrutiny. Curators
who oversee the collection and propose purchases
as well as accept gifts change over time, along with
the character of the collection.[2] While a curator's specific interest can leave a significant imprint, when he
or she leaves, these identifying characteristics are sub-
sumed by the greater and more complex compilation.
The whole becomes greater than the sum of its parts!
In time the collection becomes a living time capsule,
seen regularly in its disparate elements. Photographs
are chosen for exhibitions that are most pertinent
to the project, illustrative of a theme, or wondrous
to behold.

For *Signs of the Times* I have selected those
photographs that are, of course, pertinent to the
project, but I have also chosen images that may not
be admired for their rarity, style, or historical pedigree.
In fact, many were picked because they lacked just
those qualities. For this inquiry, a well-known photograph by Alfred Stieglitz or Edward Weston must
stand equally beside a photograph taken by a little-
known Bauhaus photographer or that of a graduate
student from The Art Institute of Chicago. Together,
it is hoped, these images will shed light upon some
of the persistent characteristics that are peculiar to the
twentieth century. What one artist looks at and com-
municates in his work is superceded by the collective
voice chanting the beliefs of the greater culture. These,
I believe, are the images that act as a visual chorus
for the notion that twentieth-century photographers
have repeated specific "objects and events"—motifs
that echo the historical condition of our time. To quote
the photographer George Tice:"…you can only see
what you are ready to see—what mirrors your mind
at that particular time."[3]

PART ONE

Photography and the modern object were inexorably linked during the first several decades of the twentieth century. Both would have been merely ideas one hundred years before. The automobile, airplane, electrical apparatus, and other mass-produced objects—as well as the industrial locations in which these things were manufactured—became subjects for the camera's lens. Indeed, the utilization of photography for the two-dimensional representation of these subjects was an affirmation, one for the other, and, at the same time, a declaration of a new order.

The coordination of iconography and style did not happen automatically. At first, photog-

ALFRED STIEGLITZ
31. *The Aeroplane*, 1910/1911

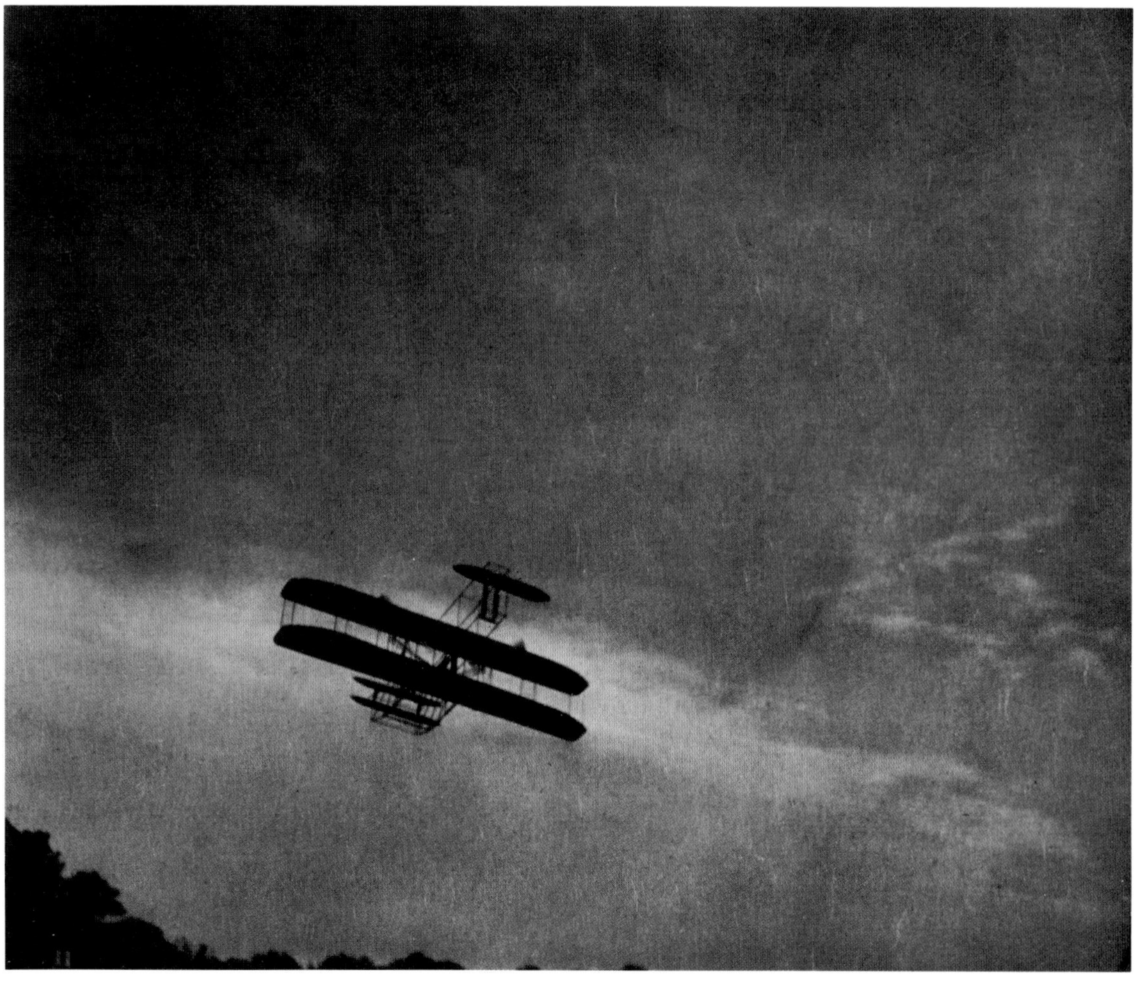

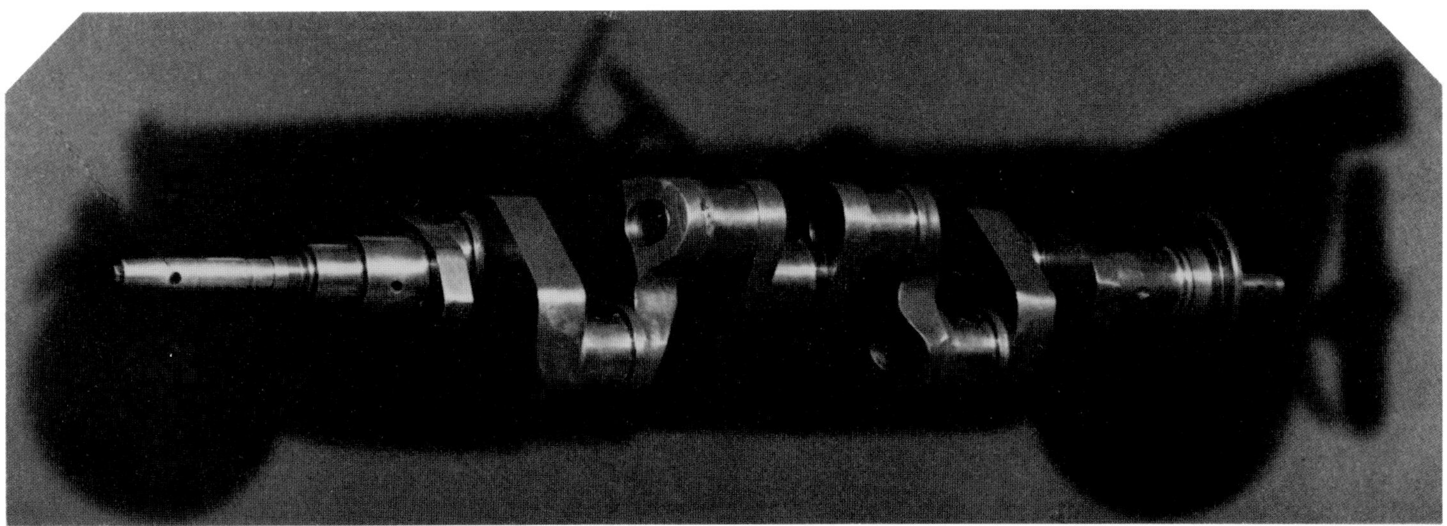

raphers, comfortable with the "look" of soft-focus pictorialism and fascinated with the changing world around them, found it awkward to incorporate the new with the old. Alfred Stieglitz, however, celebrated the new century in pictures with his series *Changing New York,* 1910. Here the old and the new meet in a common ground so that the subject matter is surrounded and softened by the haze of recognition. Stieglitz's biographer Sarah Greenough has noted that 1910 was a watershed year for Stieglitz because, "In these photographs he leapt beyond the Photo-Secession's elegies to the past…his pictures of sky-scrapers, airplanes, ferry boats, and ocean liners were icons to the twentieth century."[4] Yet in *The Aeroplane,* 1910 (cat. 31), Stieglitz's leap is hesitant, for the "aeroplane" resembles a bird soaring safely above treetops rather than clouds. The central subject, a man-made object, merely counterbalances the more traditional content…nature.

Reducing the modern object to gadget-sized proportions was one initial approach to new and unfamiliar subject matter. In Paul Outerbridge's *Crankshaft Silhouetted Against Car,* 1923 (cat. 19), the unusual and unexpected presence of a miniaturized automobile crankshaft is made to look not unlike a toy. Set against the car's silhouetted profile, the shiny metal object is situated as if we were looking through the exterior structure into the working mechanism of the automobile. Other photographers, wanting to get inside the object, moved the camera even closer to the working parts. The power of the machine's design was the impetus for their work, rather than re-creating a pastiche of parts. Paul Strand's study of the interior mechanism of a motion-picture camera, *Double Akeley, New York,* 1922 (cat. 32), and Ed Cismondi's formal confrontation with the linear configuration of an engine, *Engine Form,* 1936 (cat. 6), illustrate a determination to break into new pictorial territory. Design becomes the composition photographed so that, in the end, the subject matter is primarily a vehicle for a pictorial exercise in abstraction.

Photographs that combine the structure of an object with the presentation of the object itself tell us about its importance to our culture. By the 1930s, while the Western world suffered through an economic depression, an optimistic search for relief was sought in the

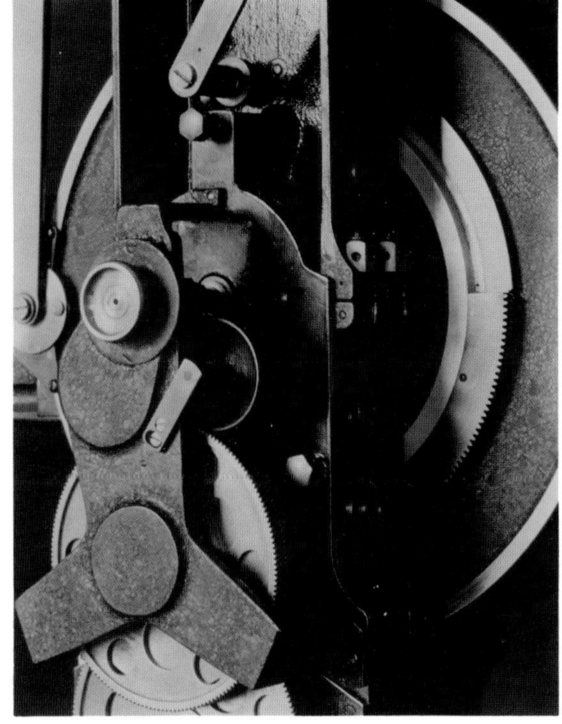

creation and distribution of new goods. These products, intended to stimulate the economy, became emblems of a fresh start in the urban landscape.

Anton Bruehl's photograph *6,000 Watts,* 1927 (cat. 4, p. 6), an homage to the ordinary lightbulb, typifies the idea of an "esthetic of progress." Repetition, illumination, finish, and the evocation of an advancing force—all part of the vocabulary of this particular photograph—are devices commonly seen in photographs of the twenties and thirties. Whether the photograph features transportation, architecture, or mass-produced products, there is a consistency of presentation when the subject matter is readily recognizable.

This consistency of presentation is readily exhibited in the European "New Vision" photography of the 1920s and early 1930s. Embracing the principles and strategies of creative invention emphasized at such design centers as the Bauhaus, photographers admired and borrowed the objects created by their peers. Their own overlay of light, composition, and vantage point was intended as a celebratory display, translating the objects into two-dimensional motifs. The automobile neatly fit their criteria as an object from the

post-war industrialized world. Moving or stationery, it became the quintessential twentieth-century subject. Not merely utilitarian, the automobile changed our quality of life, and tantalized our emotions while traveling at speeds previously unknown. No wonder it became an especially provocative motif, one that would continue to engage future generations of image-makers.

Two photographs from the 1930s celebrate the automobile in divergent fashions. Anton Stankowski's *1/100 sec bei 70 km/h,* 1930 (cat. 24), directs its attention to the emotional state, looking at the automobile in a study of fast-paced movement. The camera points toward the center of a road lined with trees that are blurred by the automobile's speed in relation to the sensitivity of film and selected shutter speed. The front end of the automobile fills the lower portion of the frame. We are thus both observer and passenger to the thrill of accelerated motion. Hein Gorny's *Untitled,* ca. 1930 (cat. 14), on the other hand, directs his image to the rational mind, showing us an elegant row of gleaming new cars. Fresh off the assembly line, these repetitive elements run diagonally across the picture plane reminiscent of the Italian Futurist construction of space-time. As in Marcel Duchamp's revolutionary painting *Nude Descending a Staircase,* 1912, Gorny has evoked movement through the configuration of completely stilled elements. Significantly, both photographers employ the devices of illuminaton and finish, coding the image with the "modern era" package. Unlike Outerbridge's see-through "mini-car," these bolder interpretations tell us as much about our attitude toward the automobile as the way it looked.

In addition to simply showing what something looked like, advertising photography thrived by promoting the invisible "idea" of the object. The more such mass-produced objects were introduced into the culture, the greater the need was to stimulate the public to consume them. Photographs, reproduced in magazines and publicity posters, could introduce and establish an aura around an otherwise unfamiliar product. Hans Finsler photographed a box of chocolates (cat. 8, p. 23). Like the automobile in Gorny's composition, each piece is a clone of the one next to it, extending the assembly-line production pictorially. Displayed in a neutral context that becomes a blank page when reproduced, the viewer (or potential consumer) can mentally recontextualize it. That is, the viewer can imagine consuming the chocolate prior to actually buying it. Using the same pictorial devices as his peers, Finsler exaggerates the smooth surface of the chocolates and arranges them in an oblique orientation to suggest an advancing force (of a hand?). Unconsciously we perceive these chocolates to be twentieth-century objects.

While architecture was one of the first subjects for the camera's lens in the nineteenth century, photography of architecture in the twentieth century is an altogether different discipline. The static formal portraits of stately mansions and government edifices recorded for posterity on salt and albumen prints were no longer suitable subjects for the new century. Photographers sought out architecture that mirrored their

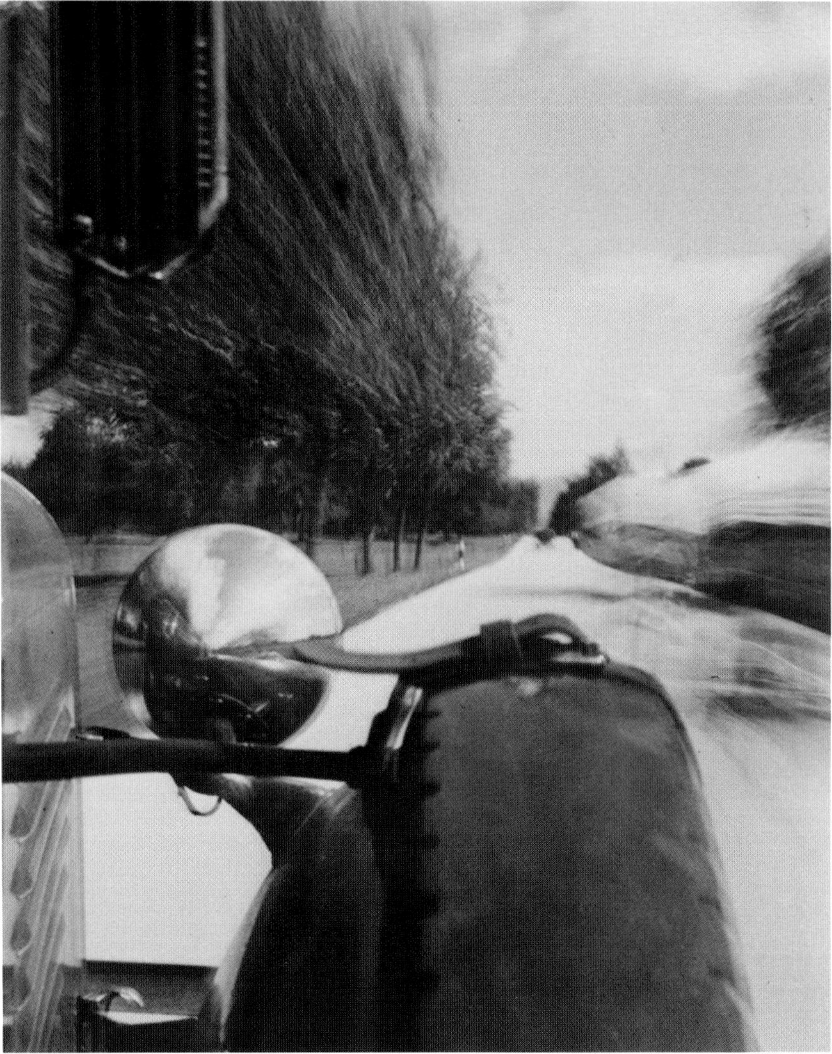

cross-disciplinary concern for form following function.
As ornate stonework was replaced by the simplicity of
steel and glass, photographers altered their approach
to the subject to accommodate the new technology
and esthetics of architecture. As buildings became
taller and clustered in urban settings, and cameras
became smaller, photographing the complete building
proved difficult. Photographers often pointed upward,
and prescribed portions of the building would stand
for the whole while simultaneously describing the
function of the building. Figural details on city halls
and churches were replaced by smokestacks on ships
and skyscrapers. Funnels, emblematic of industry itself,
became a familiar motif in contemporary photography
of the 1920s and 1930s.

Bruehl photographed a ship's funnels set against
a clear sky (cat. 5, p. 25), much like Finsler's chocolates
on a blank page. Immediately recognizable, these
architectural forms, like the curvilinear lightbulbs in
Bruehl's *6,000 Watts,* show the photographer's pre-
dilection for innate design and objects with purpose.
Brett Weston, also intrigued with industrial material,
shows his advanced sense of the arrangement of units
in Untitled *(Pipes No. 5),* 1927 (cat. 35), a study of
abstract principles rather than a presentation of pipes.
In Untitled, ca. 1932 (cat. 1, p. 26), Theo Ballmer deftly
unites both form and function in a photograph of an
interior replete with pulleys, hooks, and machines.
A negative image, the linear elements glow, illuminating
their own form while describing the parameters of the
dark interior space. Like Stankowski and Gorny's photographs that suggested the power of the automobile,
this photograph treats industrial space as a physical
subject with a sensatory presence.

These eloquent pronouncements of new things
in a new world are invested with utopian undertones.
Many exude optimism. The precision inherent in the
objects themselves and the tacit application of geom-
etry to the construction of space suggest an accuracy
which, one assumes, was intended as a hopeful attri-
bute to a better future where these products would
exist. Many of the motifs will reappear throughout
the century, but here they reveal, as Panofsky has
noted, their own historical condition. They were
created in an era that was looking for answers;
twentieth-century man's inventions were perceived
to hold the keys to those answers. Embedded in these
photographs are most certainly the beliefs and
dreams of that era.

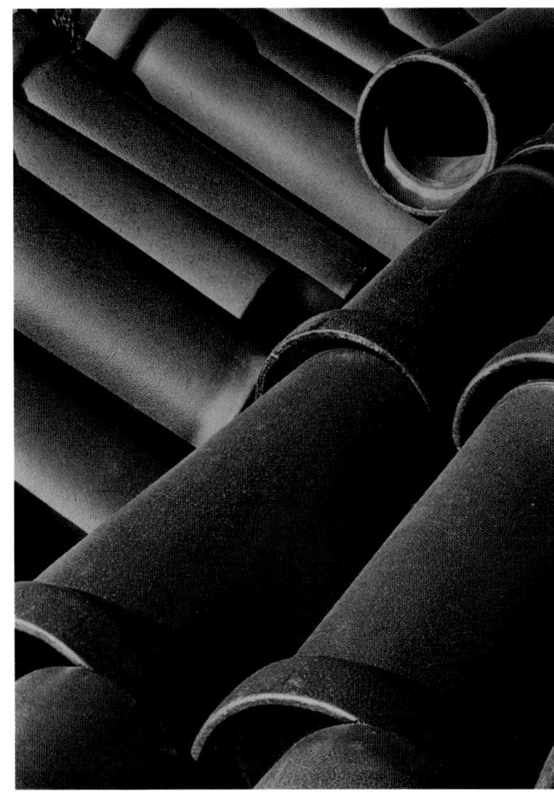

BRETT WESTON
35. Untitled *(Pipes No. 5),* 1927

The Disembodied Human Figure

The esteem in which artists held the machine and the modern object in the 1920s and 1930s was countered by a fascination with the human figure as a popular motif. The emotional component, touched upon in Anton Stankowski's photograph of a speeding automobile (cat. 24, p. 10), found fuller expression in the motif of the disembodied figure. Seemingly irrational, the image of an unconnected hand, leg, or face found refuge in the language of Surrealism. These human motifs, oriented toward the unconscious mind rather than toward images designed to invoke a possible future machine-filled world, were intended to mystify and disconcert. These figural landscapes were found only in the the the furthest reaches of the collective imagination of artists, not in the coherent dreams of designers and visual thinkers.

Surrealist-inspired photographs changed the role of photography. For eighty years, photographs were meant to explain clearly, to describe succinctly, so that questions were answered, not asked. By the 1920s photographs could enter into the realm of the illogical—like literature they were infested with implication as well as description. Often placed with other objects or appearing in reasonless situations, the disembodied human figure disclaimed the more optimistic presentation of a world surrounded with shiny new consumer products. In many of these photographs, the disjointed limbs and body parts mirrored the displacement of society between the two world wars.

To suggest that these irregular forms were found solely in the medium of photography would be untrue. Indeed, artists employed them in collages, paintings, and ready-mades, popular experimental sculptures made from found objects. But the application of the illogical motif in a photograph is certainly more compelling. A continuous-tone image made with a mixture of lens, light, and photo-chemistry without the aid of manual intervention is usually mistaken for the truth. Photography plays on our disbelief of the disguise, and so we accept the implausible as fact.

Hands are like living beings. Only Servants?
Possibly. Servants, then, with a vigorous
free spirit, with a physiognomy. Eyeless and
voiceless faces which nonetheless see and speak.
Henri Focillon[5]

In 1936, the art historian Henri Focillon wrote "In Praise of Hands," a final essay to conclude the second edition of his renowned philosophical treatise, *The Life Forms of Art.* The metaphor of the hand was used to celebrate handwork and to denigrate the evolving role of mechanical means in the production of works of art. No longer were the tasks dictated by the eye and mind dutifully carried out solely by the hand.

The literary symbol had been a familiar one in the vocabulary of Surrealism. While the hand had disappeared (in Focillon's opinion) from its primary position in the creation of art, it appeared as a motif instead. In photography, the very medium Focillon may have alluded to in his essay, the motif of the disembodied hand often appears like an "unconscious act." Autonomous, it moves over the picture plane with a "mind of its own," emancipated from its servitude to the ego. One wonders if the experience of working on an assembly line or with industrial machinery which required rapid, repetitive movement of the hands might have generated a reason for this particular motif.

Man Ray especially favored the motif of the hand in his work and used it in a variety of ways. It appeared as a four-fingered shadow in a photogram, a mannequin hand in a ready-made, and as a hand-print stamped in vivid color on a painting. In the Museum's photography collection, there is a 1933

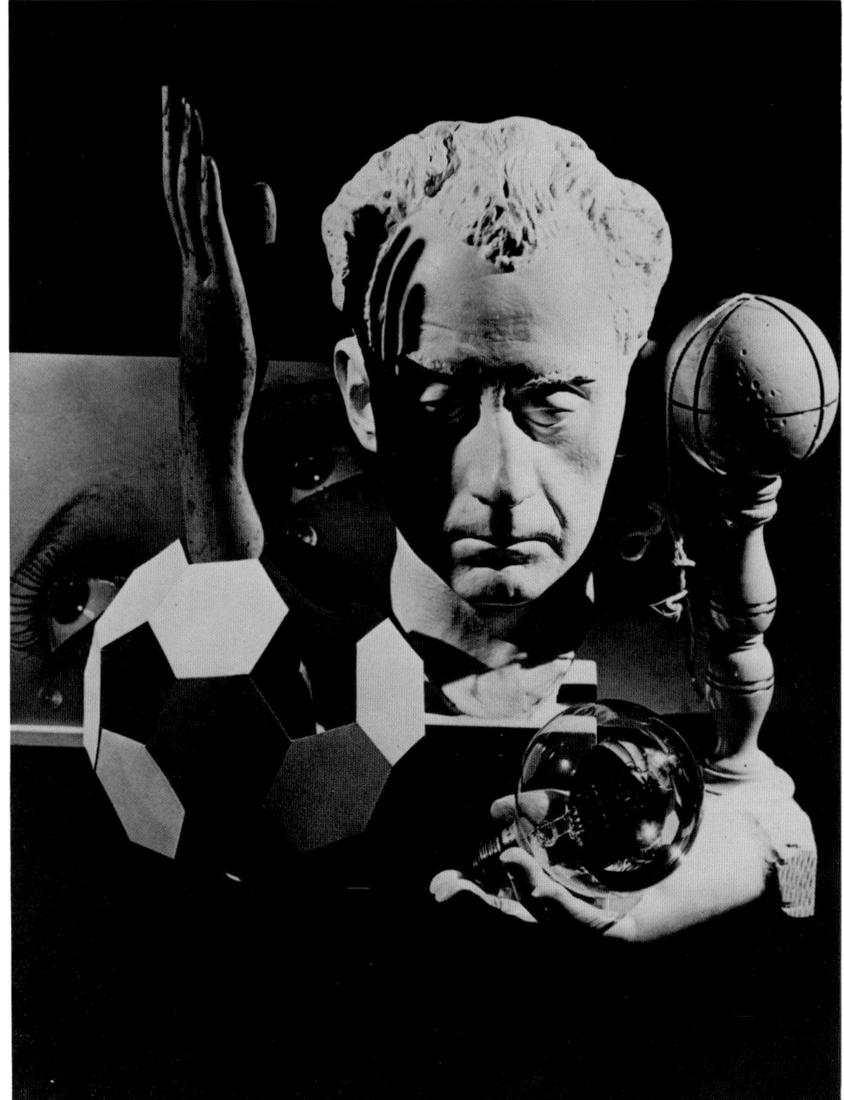

self-portrait of the artist (cat. 87). His likeness is represented by a sculpted head, possibly made from a plaster casting, surrounded by an array of objects, including a lightbulb, polyhedron, and two plaster hands. Both *objets trouve*, one was originally used as a glove display prop in a retail store. While the viewer ponders the significance of each of the objects in the arrangement, the presence of two hands is indeed central to the picture's poetic content. Could, as Focillon suggests, the motif make reference to the artist's independent, creative spirit? Indeed the prevalence of the hand motif in Man Ray's work has prompted the suggestion that he used it to refer to himself in a kind of visual pun. The French word for hand is *main* pronounced like the artist's first name with less emphasis on the final consonant.[6]

When juxtaposed among other objects, the disembodied hand suggests a need for resolution. For example, in an untitled Rayograph from 1922 (cat. 85), Man Ray shows us the shadowy remnant of four fingers next to that of a dangling key and a food grater. Roger Parry creates a parallel juxtaposition of a limp hand lying next to a smoldering gun in a ca. 1929 photograph from the book *Banalité*. In both instances the objects generate the notion of action for an unseen event. Food graters, keys, and guns are objects requiring direct manual involvement to be activated. Separated from the rest of the body (read: brain), the hand, we assume, has again acted on its own… to some illogical conclusion. Here the independent spirit, possibly an evil one, is further implied by the somber dark tones.

There is an explicit connection between the hand and thimble in Alfred Stieglitz's famous photograph from what was an ongoing series of portraits of Georgia O'Keeffe (cat. 100). We can infer that these hands are involved in the creative act of sewing. Moreover, O'Keeffe's hands have become recognized emblems for the woman herself, almost as familiar as portraits of her face. They have taken on the role of equivalents for the particular person. The implicit message conveyed in the photograph is the same as that found in Man Ray's self-portrait. Both convey the idea that the active, creative spirit is the subconscious secret codified in the disembodied hand. Even Henry Swift's Untitled, 1930s (cat. 104, p. 33), an innocent study of a hand and its shadow playing with a wire Slinky toy, invokes the notion of the creative spirit released from constraints. Acting without benefit of mind or body, the hands dance with the object, performing a *pas de deux* for the camera.

While the hand motif appears to symbolize the active and creative attributes of man, the motif of fragmented legs appears to be that of the mindless and passive receptacle. They are generally female legs, often rendered as static entities, going nowhere with no intent or purpose. Perhaps they stand for the direction of society as seen by artists of the years between the two world wars. One of Hans Bellmer's bizarre studies from 1936 of a mannequin from the cult classic *La Poupée* (cat. 43), for example, could support this proposition. Twisted into a confined posture, the lower trunk and legs of the mannequin invite

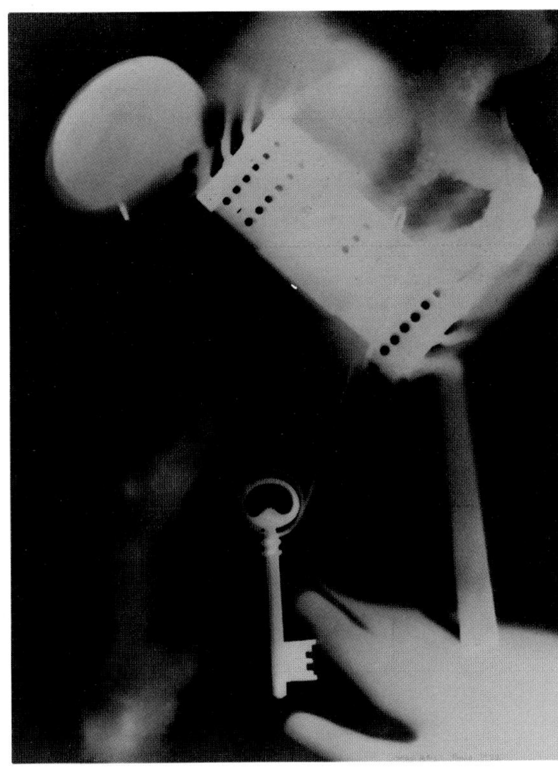

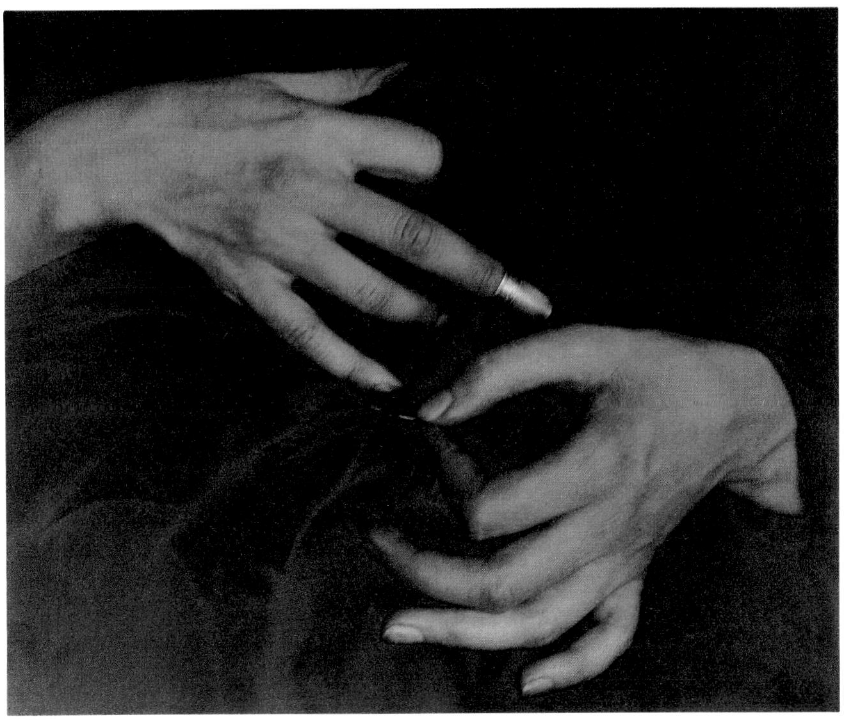

only the suggestion of sexual innuendo. Less static, but equally seductive, is Umbo's *Pantoffeln*, ca. 1928-29 (cat. 110, p. 14). Again, the motif is rendered as a mannequin's legs and, although standing, they are shod in backless bedroom slippers, accentuating their erotic intent while confirming that the legs will hardly be able to run very fast or far.

Stieglitz's version of the motif, employing the feet and legs of Katherine Dudley (cat. 102), particularizes the sexual implication. The crossed position of her legs hints at a hesitancy in the message, yet, bare legs and sandaled feet in the 1920s were not a sign of prudishness. Women began wearing shorter skirts baring what had once been hidden behind ankle-

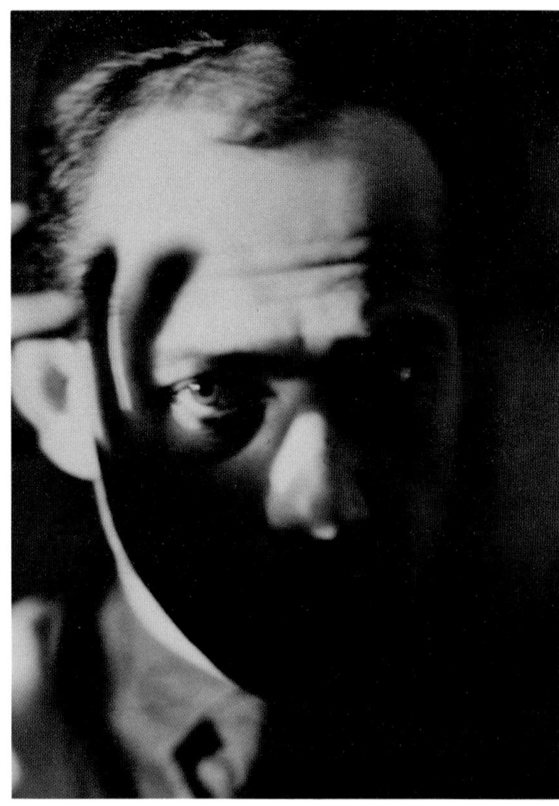

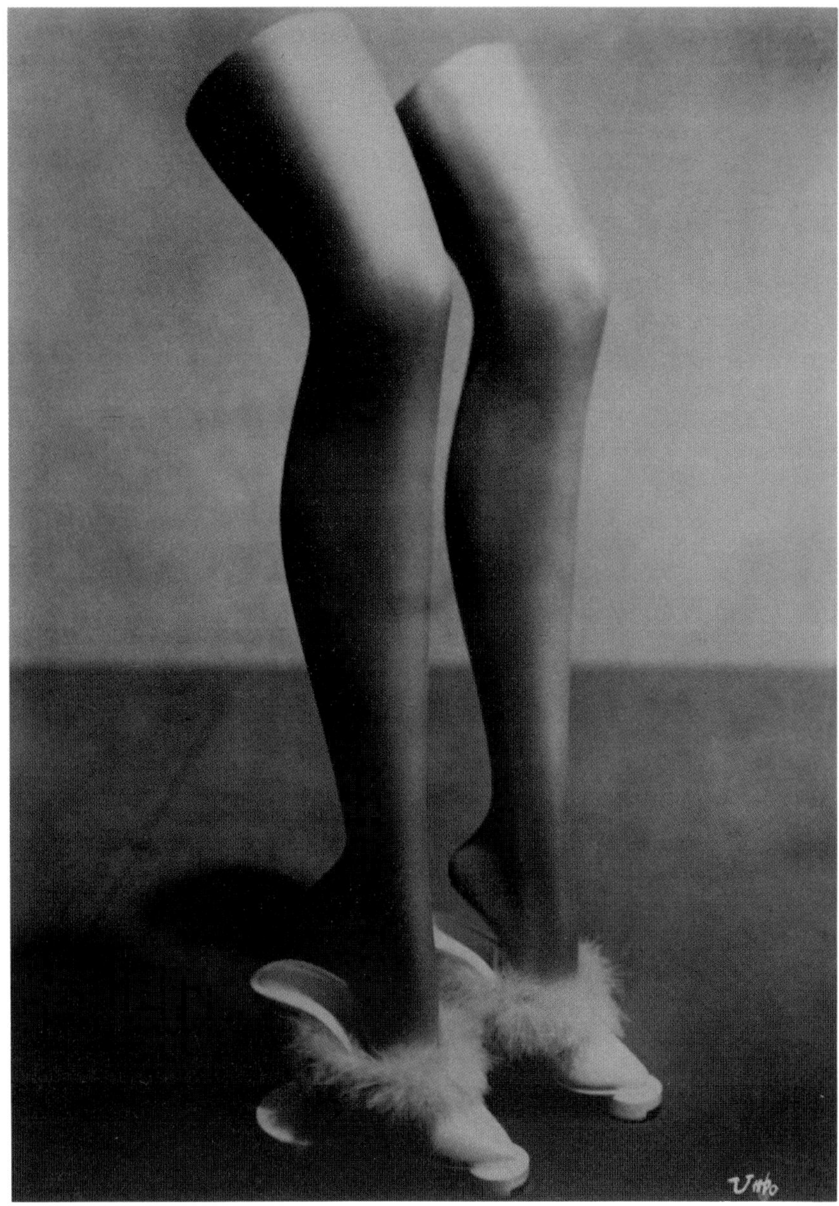

length dresses. New fashions gave women physical freedom which paralleled the suffragette movement of the era. The interaction between the photographer and the subject, a major theme in Stieglitz's oeuvre, could be perceived here as one supplying mixed messages: Dudley's posture is both inviting and resisting.

Fragmented legs, whether from a living figure or a mannequin, are also found in photographed situations of complete scenes. Manuel Alvarez Bravo finds the motif in an advertisement displaying a pair of legs painted on the side of a building. In *Dos Pares de Piernas*, 1928-29 (cat. 40, p. 29), a man and woman's legs are highlighted by a pair of electric lights illuminating the billboard beneath another pair of windows. Barely visible at the bottom of the frame is the word "inimitable." Perhaps Alvarez Bravo is commenting on the obstacles of coupling, almost as if he had observed the dilemma depicted in Stieglitz's photograph of Katherine Dudley's feet.

The most prevalent motif of the human figure is, of course, the face. While usually the key body part in traditional portraiture, the faces of the twenties and thirties tended to be discrete, masklike shapes rather than volumetric forms describing the head connected to the body. Often the face is isolated from the torso, a bodiless entity floating in weightless space. While today we recognize this type of portraiture as a rational formal arrangement, its appearance in the 1920s and 1930s registered a fundamental shift from the standard representation of the human visage in photography. Previously, photographic portraits conveyed as much information as possible. The sitter was placed to show costume, setting, and often such objects as books, pens, or flowers that lent further associative knowledge to our understanding of the subject. By the 1920s, however, all pictorial attributes were stripped away. Few of the faces show strong expressions; most stare blankly at the camera or out somewhere beyond the frame. If eyes are windows to the soul, then in these photographs the soul is a blank slate. This blankness de-particularizes the person being photographed while estheticizing the pictorial structure.

Other schematic devices serve to underscore the independence of the face as a motif. Darkness, for instance, obscuring the eyes, further holds back any clues to the personality of the sitter. Umbo uses this device repeatedly in his work. In his self-portrait *Selbst*, ca. 1930 (cat. 111, p. 47), he shields his eyes with dark glasses and the silhouette of his camera forms a pattern above his nose. The photograph then becomes an iconographical contradiction: his sight is obscured, but the motif of the camera implies a second vision.

In the same year, the Italian Futurist Tato (Guglielmo Sansoni) obscured the photographically "decapitated" head of poet Remo Chiti with the superimposition of the image of a clock's inner mechanism (cat. 107). Intended to define the sitter's personality, the imagery employed confronts rather than suggests whereas in an earlier era, for example, he might have been portrayed holding a clock. Equally mysterious is Marianne Bresslauer's ca. 1927 portrait of the painter Paul Citroen (cat. 53). The shadow of his own hand shields his face that is submerged in a dark back-

ground. Here, perhaps, two twentieth-century motifs
come into play: the hand, the creative component;
and the face, the mask of the soul.

Commercial portrait photographers borrowed much
of the vocabulary of the disembodied face because
it fit so easily into the realm of modern portraiture.
The blank stare that was originally intended to disas-
sociate the sitter and his or her likeness now became
the *haute posture* of nonchalance for the celebrated.
In a ca. 1930-33 portrait of Douglas Fairbanks (cat. 66,
p. 39) by George Hurrell, Fairbanks appears indifferent
to the cries of adulation from his fans and distances
himself from his imagined audience by assuming this
psychological stance. Hurrell also borrows the device
of severing the face from the body and surrounding
it with objects of near-equal size, similar to Man Ray's
self-portrait. Whereas the unusual objects in Man Ray's
photograph are meant to purposely confuse, those
in Hurrell's portrait of Fairbanks are more traditionally
employed. Like objects found in nineteenth-century
portraiture, they are intended to imbue the sitter with
such qualities as taste and wisdom.

In Germany, Lotte Jacobi built a reputation photographing the celebrated figures of her day, not unlike
that of Hurrell in Hollywood. Van Deren Coke has
noted Jacobi's direct appropriation of motifs from
European "New Vision" photographers. He writes:
"She 'styled' her portraits by directing the lights to suggest a mask over the face of her subjects. This sense
of stage drama was accentuated by the cinematic
device of moving in close or placing the face off center.…she seems to have independently embodied in her
work, accents such as this, to create what were thought

of as modern portraits."[7]

These motifs, utilized for a broad range of personal and commercial work, seemed especially appro-
priate in an era circumscribed by two world wars.
Indeed, the fragmented nature of these forms mirrored
the political and economic unrest that characterized
the times. That the motifs would continue to maintain
their currency for another half century is the topic
considered in Part II.

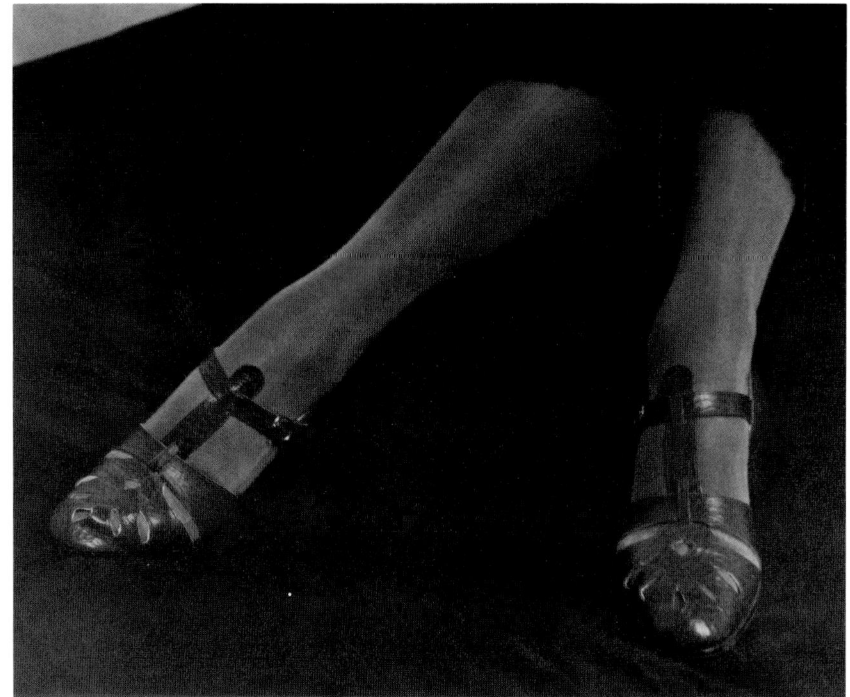

PART TWO

By the time the Second World War broke out in Europe in September 1939, many artists had escaped the continent for England and the United States. With them, they took the ideas, style, and language of the art of their generation; for most of them that meant Surrealism. In exile, exhibitions of paintings, drawings, and sculpture disseminated their work to a new public and perpetuated the emblems of Surrealism to a younger generation.[8] The motifs made sense. They were conceived in a world not dissimilar to that of the 1940s and early 1950s—a world embroiled in and recuperating from another world war.

It is probable that Aaron Siskind, for instance, was introduced to the paintings of Surrealism in New York in the early 1940s. The vocabulary of bizarre juxtapositions and pieces of the human figure placed in compositions as if they were ordinary household objects appeared translatable into photography. The legacy of Surrealist photographers, on the other hand, was less known, for the medium still did not garner the attention of most gallery and museum directors.[9] Siskind, however, incorporated the motif of the isolated hand in his work in the early 1940s. His most successful treatment of it appeared in the photograph *Gloucester I,* 1944, (cat. 180), in which an abandoned work glove took on the proportions of a limp hand while lying against the weather-worn wood of an old wharf. As photographed, the grain of the wood translates into that of a wall, and the glove reaches out to captivate all who behold it. The formidable, independent, and creative spirit, laced with the mystery implied by the motif in an earlier decade, has now changed. Independence has become isolation, and the engaging spirit of creativity has altered into a state of subtle anxiety. Carl Chiarenza, Siskind's biographer, has noted that the image spoke eloquently to an audience that immediately recognized their own sense of concern and despair at the world in the empty work glove feebly attempting to reach out beyond the frame.[10]

Without musculature, the hand, shown in a shallow, finite space, has a godlike presence, as if only the divine spirit itself could generate volume in a flat form. Indeed, a disembodied hand hanging like a light

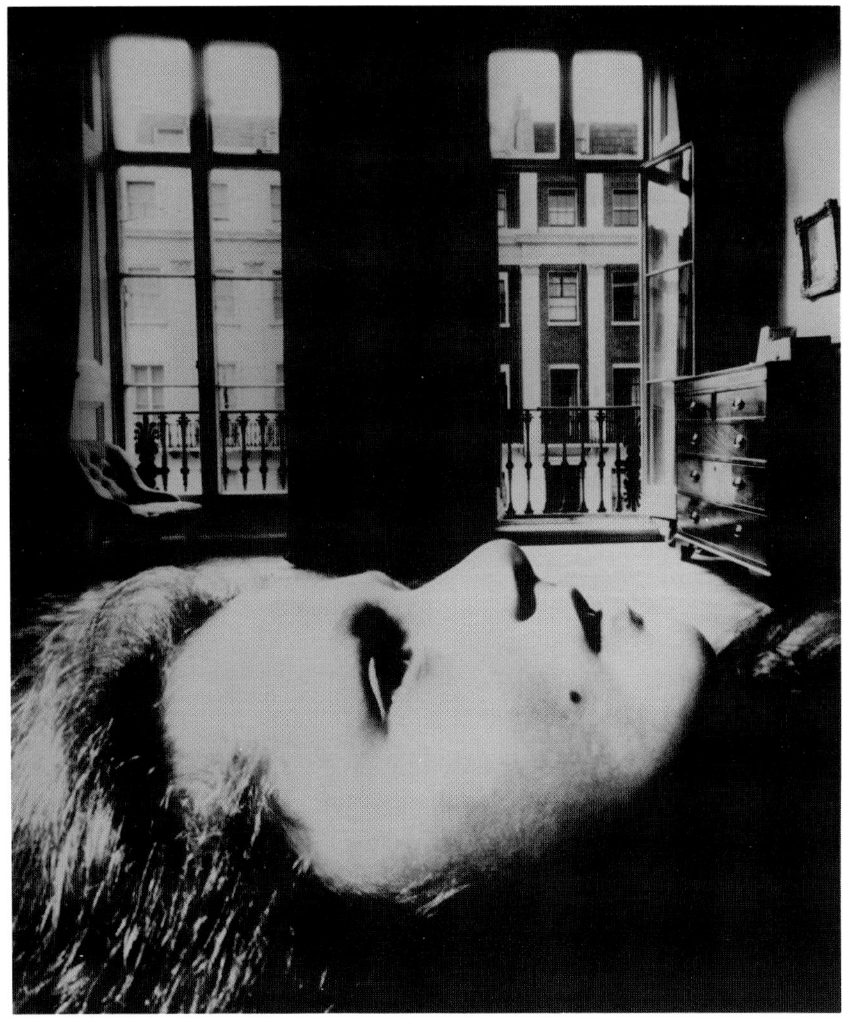

fixture from the upper frame of a painting often stood
for the manifestation of God's presence in Christian
iconography. Without specific textual references
in contemporary art, there is no way to explain
the iconography, but, as we have seen, this particular
motif has become a permanent addition to the visual
language of twentieth-century photography.

Even in the 1960s, when the hallmark of art photography was work which assumed principles of vernac-
ular photography, and the snapshot was the stylistic
role model, the hand appears as a motif. Attempting
to divorce themselves from achievements in other
media (as well as those in photography's history),
photographers believed that the medium would only
be recognized in the art world if the formal criteria
peculiar to it were practiced. William Klein approached
his work in this way, gathering together time, vantage
point, light, and the frame into a type of photography
that appears to be iconoclastic—— little of the traditional approaches to subject matter and composition
is evident. But in *Hand, Lebanon,* 1963 (cat. 151), Klein
has sliced off the arm of a figure with the frame of his
35mm camera and used the motif to "disarm" the
viewer. The gravity-defying appendage in no way
indicates the spiritual presence of a supreme being
praising the depicted event. Rather it is the "hands off"
gesture of a physically superior being denouncing
the photographic act taking place. God has become
an angry man.

As in the work of the first-generation photographers,
the motif in all its different guises—as glove, mannequin, human hand, or disembodied face—persists
and has become a permanent fixture in our era.
That much of its hypnotic content has become diluted
with time only confirms its accepted place in the collective subconscious of contemporary image-makers.
The creative portrait has become the standard.

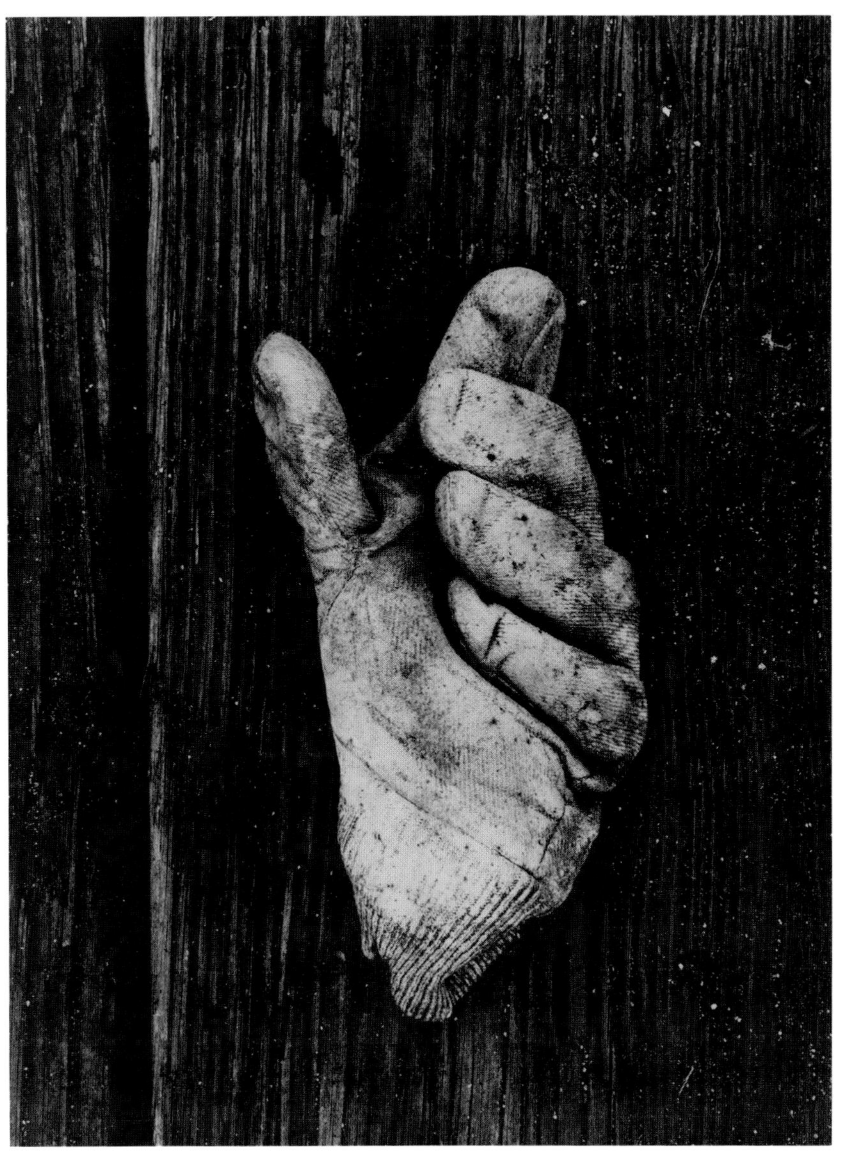

AARON SISKIND
180. *Gloucester I,* 1944

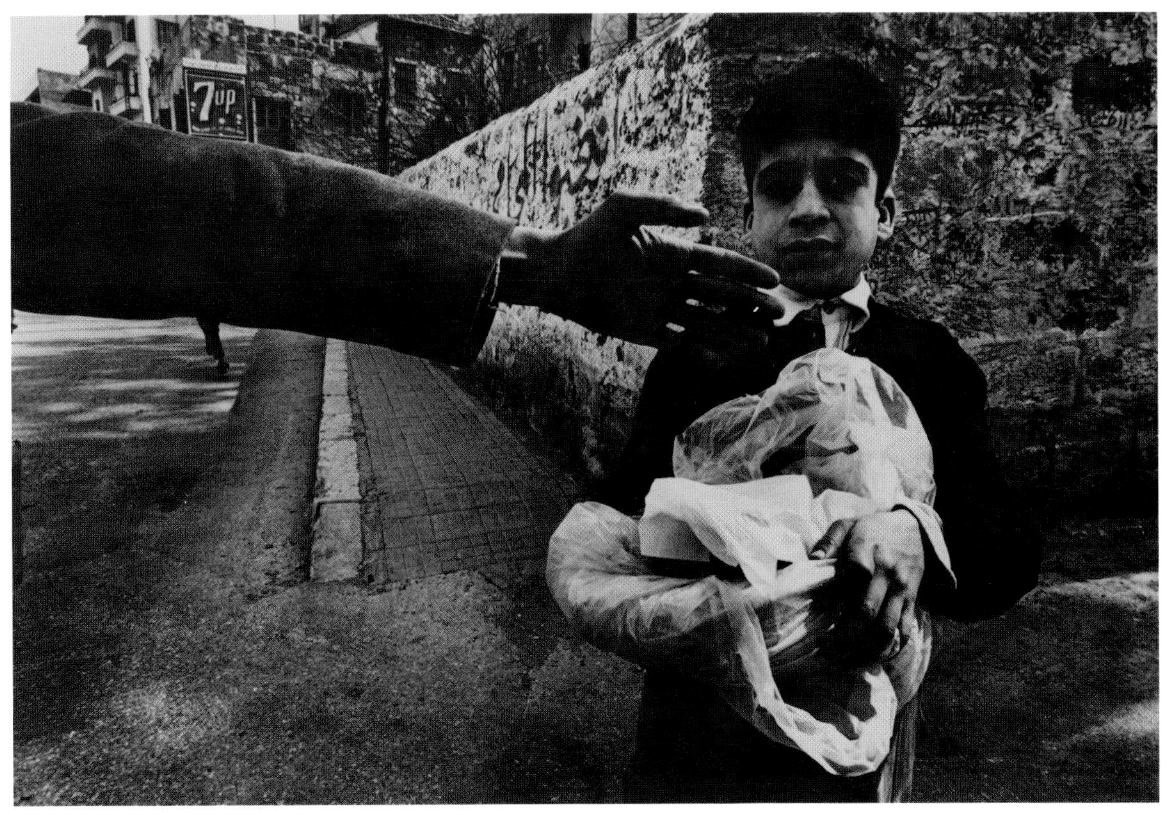

WILLIAM KLEIN
151. *Hand, Lebanon,* 1963/1980

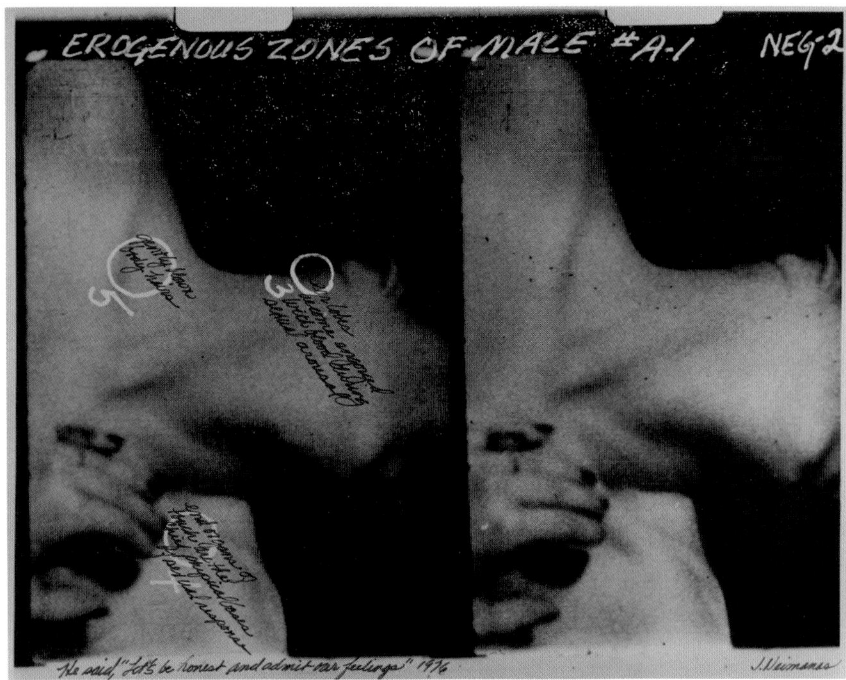

Bill Brandt, for instance, uses a child's face to exploit scale. In *Portrait of a Young Girl (Eaton Place, London)*, 1955 (cat. 125, p. 17), the photographer pits an overpowering profile against the miniscule interior space of a background. The three walls squeeze the face in the foreground out toward the viewer. Brandt's concerns are with the description of an unusual space; the face is merely a device for realizing that description. Similar to Brandt's description of a psychological space, Lee Friedlander traps a child's face inside a television set (cat. 136). Both are curious about the depiction of isolation, but Friedlander underscores his concern with a technological motif, the television set.

By the 1970s, the configuration of the motif itself, rather than any implicit meaning within it, was the challenge. Forms were there only for their own sake; later performance became the underlying impetus. Larry Sultan (cat. 186, p. 41), and Bruce Patterson (cat. 173, p. 41), may have been interested in the way photographic material translated water against flesh or dark curly hair into a photograph, but other artists were even less concerned about the way things looked photographed. Harold Jones's photograph of his face set against harsh sunlight while showering (cat. 150) becomes somewhat like a document of a particular performance. Joyce Neimanas selected frames from a pornographic film to illustrate a handwritten overlay of quotations from Masters and Johnson's *Human Sexual Response* (cat. 169). The two frames imply the cinematic origin of the forms. One can easily assume that it is the portrayal rather than the portrait that is being relayed in the photograph.

If we reexamine the three figural motifs, the legs seem to be of most interest to post-World War I photographers. Dance immediately comes to mind. The legs depicted in the 1930s appear static rather than active, and in the 1940s some were imaged as stumps rather than as graceful limbs. Weegee understood the

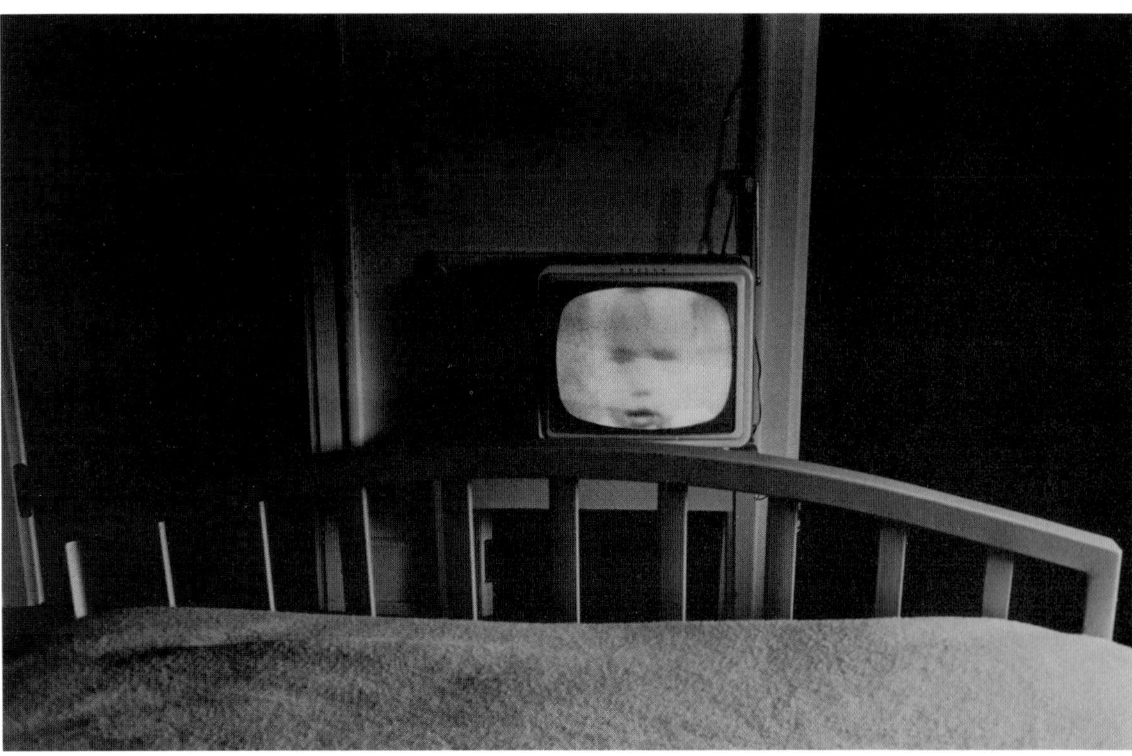

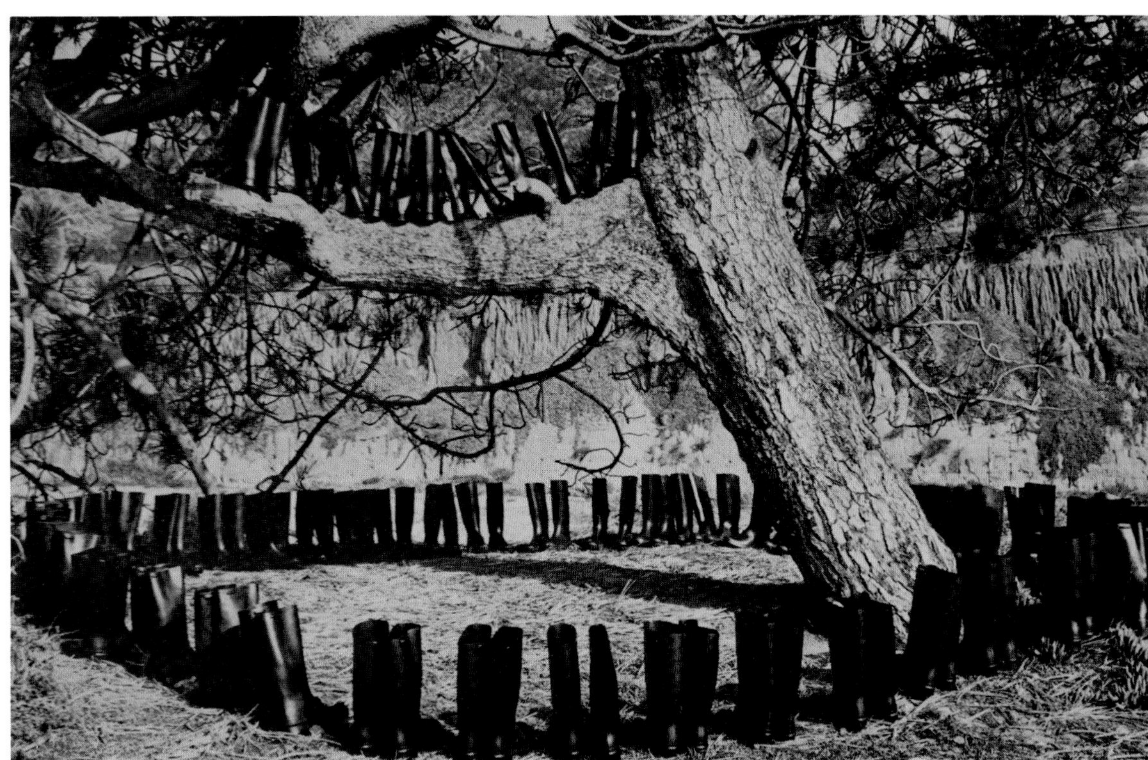

associations we tend to make with this motif, so he pulls the rug out from under our expectations. In *Bowery Savings Bank*, 1944 (cat. 199), he shows us the over-stuffed, broken-down leg of an old woman who has hidden money in her stocking. The gesture of her leg, poised like a ballerina, mocks both the gesture and the motif. Frederick Sommer, like Weegee, purposely reuses familiar motifs to twist our memory of them. In an untitled photograph from 1950 (cat. 184, p. 28), Sommer couples doll legs with the scene of a car in front of a house. With eyeballs on top of them, the legs have been reversed so that they seem stuck in an unnatural position. Overlayed is a photographically pitted surface to suggest that the whole scene is disin-tegrating. Along with Weegee, Sommer exaggerates the motif of the seductive leg and turns it back on itself in a mocking statement.

By the 1970s, all of these motifs had little currency as emblems. Not as popular as the isolated face or fragmented hands, legs and feet appeared even less frequently in photographs. Eleanor Antin made use of one hundred boots in an ongoing series from 1971 to 1973 (cat. 122). Conceptually oriented, she organized the boots in various locales and situations, had them photographed, and then made into postcards which she sent through the mail. While her intent may have been to spoof the postcard, she joins a long tra-dition of artists who have used clothing as a stand-in for the figure. Like Siskind's glove, Antin's shoes com-mand our attention. But here we laugh along with her at the tongue-in-cheek use of the motif. By now we have become immune to the use of the motif of human disembodied parts, so that its use has become bank-rupt in terms of carrying with it angst, sexual suggestion, or even the weight of "modernity." As it became a hol-low form, the twentieth-century object reappeared to take its place in the continuing discourse between the medium and subject matter.

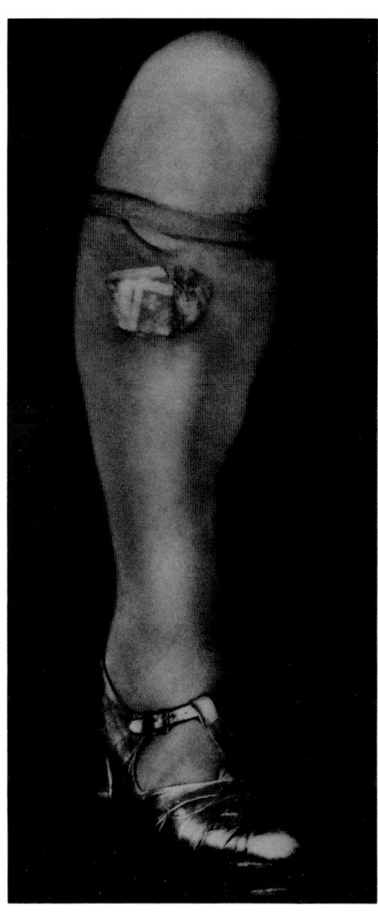

The Twentieth-Century Object—
A Perspective from the Final Decades

By the late 1960s, serious questions were being asked about the accepted rules of photography. Historians were noting that the perfect black-and-white print, the legacy of Ansel Adams and the f.64 movement, was giving way to a Pandora's box of photographic practices. Mixed-media, multi-media, and nonsilver techniques were the novel directions of many photographers from the academic arena. The universities were instrumental in incorporating photography with other liberal- and fine-arts disciplines, and shortly the black-and-white print was seen as an example of conservatism.

Less than a decade later, however, these rebellious approaches wore out. The esthetics of photographic practice broadened, but the spoils from the battle were small. As it became acceptable to draw on a negative or print, enlarge it, and print it as a cyanotype, it became less interesting to do so. Process was no longer a forbidden fruit. Subject matter, the most compelling component in photography, had not changed substantially with the barrage of new processes. By the late seventies a growing roster of photographers began to reevaluate traditional subjects, but with cynical eyes.

It seemed that by the late 1970s the entire world and everything in it had been documented by the photograph; that many of the same objects which had interested a generation of photographers in the 1920s and 1930s were again being recalled for use as subject matter. Objects, however, have appeared in virtually every type of twentieth-century photograph—snapshots, industrial photography, editorial photography, and even "art photography." Automobiles and jukeboxes, for example, were the leitmotif in Robert Frank's photographic epic of mid-century, *The Americans.* In them he saw the degeneration of the American way of life. The objects of conspicuous consumption codified the ills of society. As part of the contemporary landscape, these, and other twentieth-century objects, supplied details and anchored the photographs to a specific time or place. But as subjects in their own right, they had not seen center stage since the Constructivist heyday, when objects themselves held the attention of and were intently observed by photographers and their public. Their "newness" perhaps instigated their intense scrutiny.

Things changed. The automobile, for example, became a ubiquitous part of the urban environment, so much so, in fact, that it was hardly ever noticed anymore. Products of industry and technology were taken for granted and were seldom considered after they left the showroom floor. By the mid-seventies, when the ordinary object again became of interest to a new generation, it was seen differently, with a demoralized demeanor instead of a utopian one. Your future, as the saying goes, isn't what it used to be.

James Hajicek's 1979 untitled photograph of lightbulbs and electrical apparatus (cat. 220, p. 7) is in technological disarray. In only a half century, order and sleekness have given way to chaos and coarseness. Hajicek has, it appears, invalidated Anton Bruehl's regal, visionary procession of lightbulbs. Now they are merely burnt-out shells that reveal their inherent limitations.

As disturbing as Jo Ann Callis's *Still Life with Lobster,* 1983 (cat. 219) is, the apparent order in the juxtaposition of objects in four equal quadrants belies the underlying cerebral confusion of what still lifes are about. Callis uses what she calls "generic" objects to trigger the viewer's memory mechanism. Neither the object nor the photographer's "sculpting" them with the camera is Callis's concern. Instead she labors to present the objects with such an intensity of perception that they "verify their own authenticity."[11] Callis leads us to her picture, but refuses to tell us what to think as she is trying to change the notion of the artist's role in the three-way conversation that takes place between artist, photograph, and

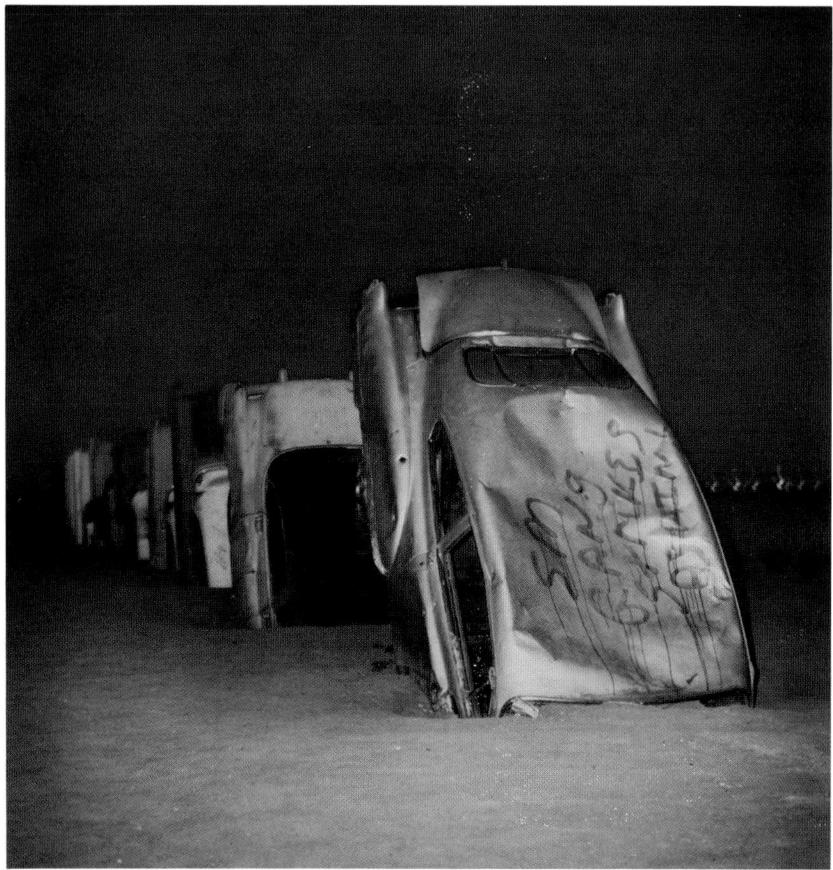

ROBERT A. WIDDICOMBE
226. *Cadillac Ranch, Amarillo, Texas,* 1979 (created by Art Farm, 1974)

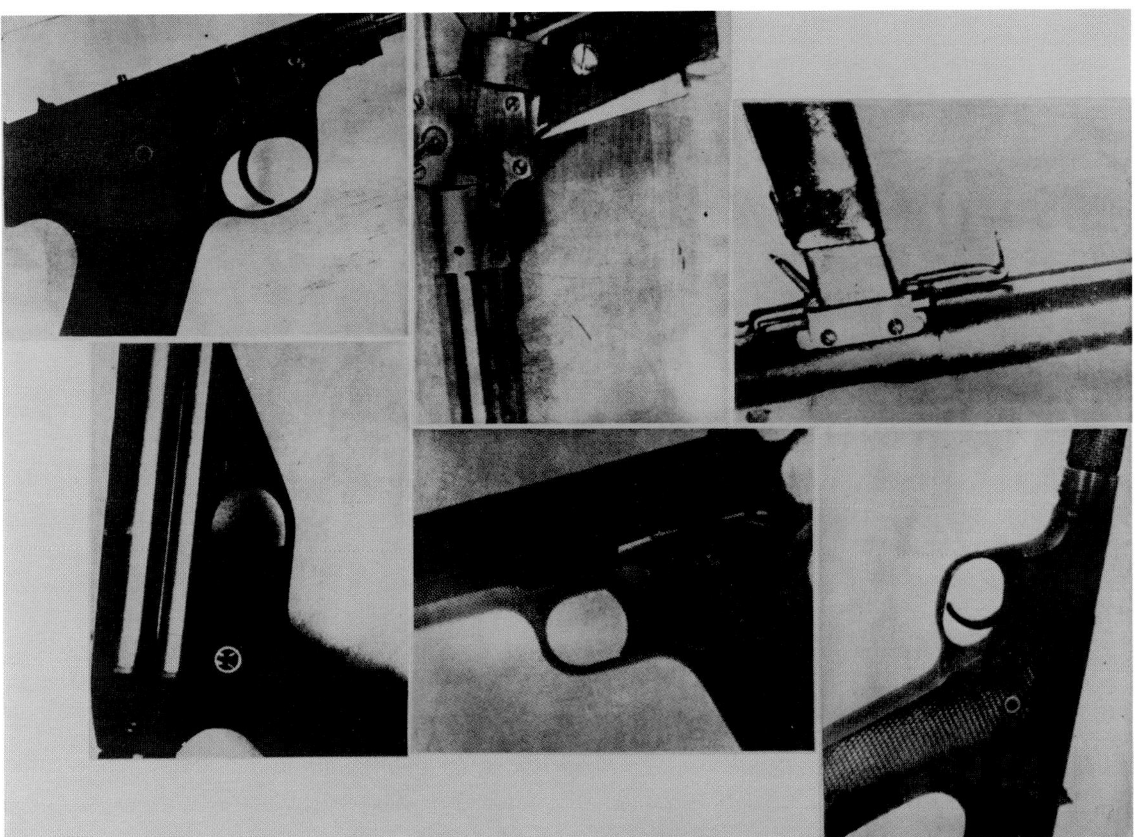

the viewer. That these images unbalance some belief system in each of us is Callis's goal.

Vito Acconci is clearly more direct in his confrontation with his audience's collective psyche. The subtitle for *Bite the Bullet: Slow Guns for Quick Sale,* 1977 (cat. 211), is: *To Be Etched on Your American Mind.* What is probably already "etched" is a random display of handguns, the kind that are easy to obtain in our culture. Acconci's photo-etching is about the destructive inclination of our society which allows the violent killing of more people per year by firearms than by catastrophic diseases.

Even more pointed is Robert Widdicombe's luscious still life, *Cadillac Ranch, Amarillo, Texas,* 1979 (cat. 226), composed of the buried ends of more than a half-dozen late-model automobiles. Cataloging not only the changing style of the Cadillac but also planned obsolescence, the photograph speaks eloquently about the automobile's real legacy. The beauty in Hein Gorny's gleaming line-up of brand-new cars (cat. 14), or Anton Stankowski's homage to speed (cat. 24, p. 10), has decayed over the decades into the reality of highway deaths, more than the American casualties from both world wars. Widdicombe's special brand of color, metallic in an electric field of blue, seems like a dream image; he gives us a view from behind rose-colored glasses.

The shift in photography's tone in the last seventy years has gone through considerable changes in spite of the constancy of its motifs. The promise of technology that appeared so forthrightly in early twentieth-century images is now being reexplored by the caustic eyes of contemporary image-makers. The disembodied human figure that confused and titillated audiences from the 1920s to the 1950s has become more or less meaningless. Today these motifs are read simply as

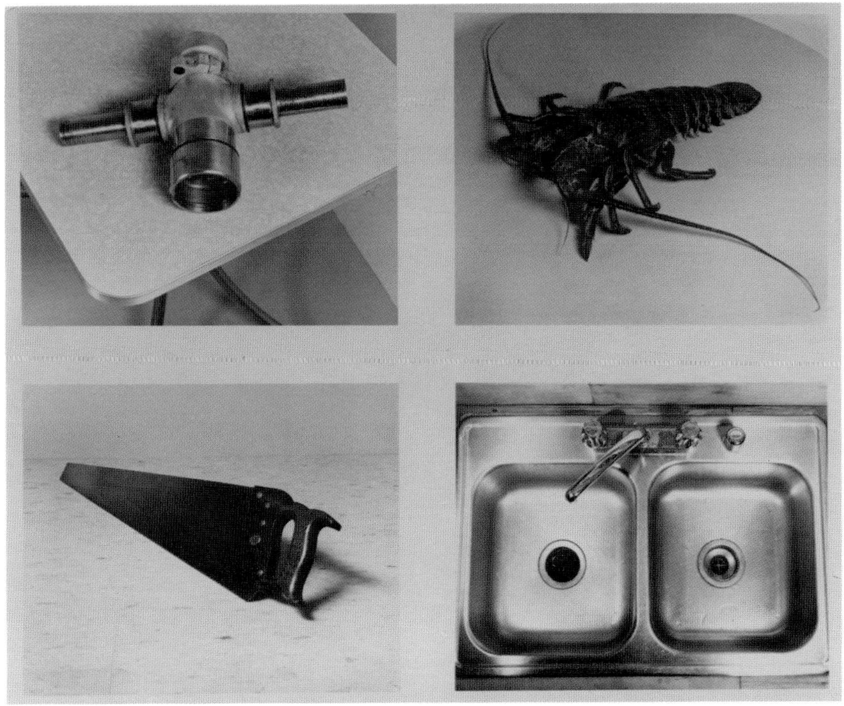

elements of composition devoid of powerful or provocative association. Is the dour tenor of contemporary photography the result of an ongoing pessimism that has afflicted our age? Is it the creative manifestation of an end-of-millenium malaise? Perhaps.

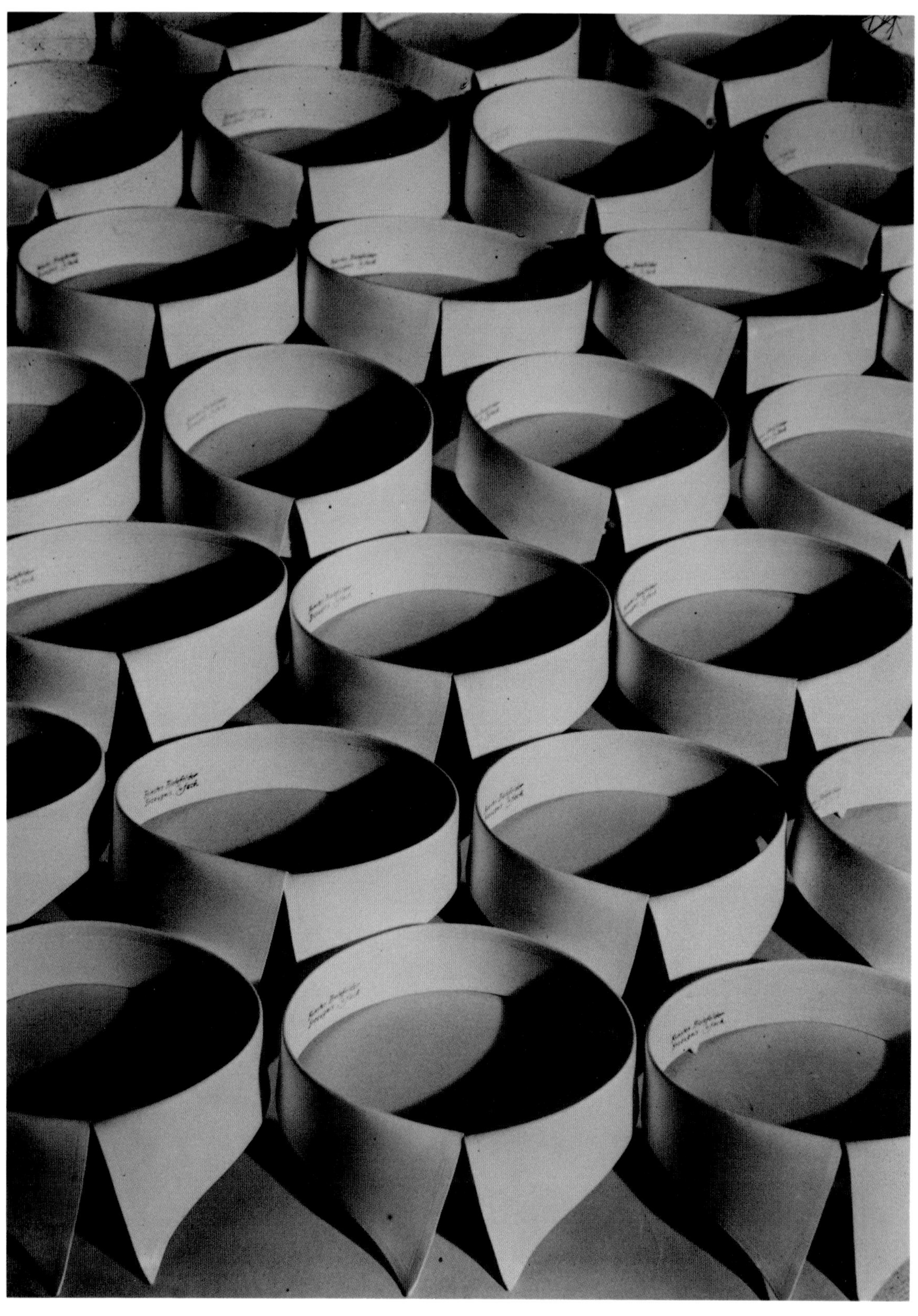

HEIN GORNY
13. Untitled, 1928/1980

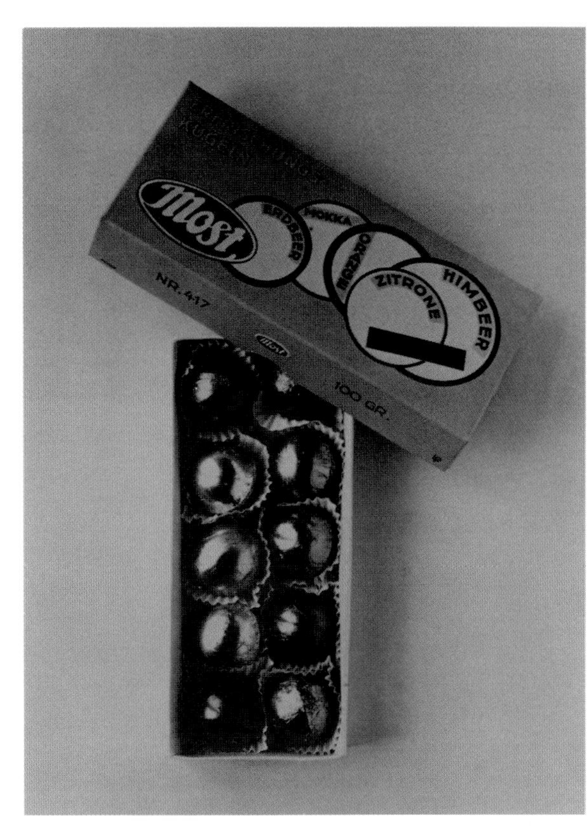

HANS FINSLER
8. Untitled, 1920s

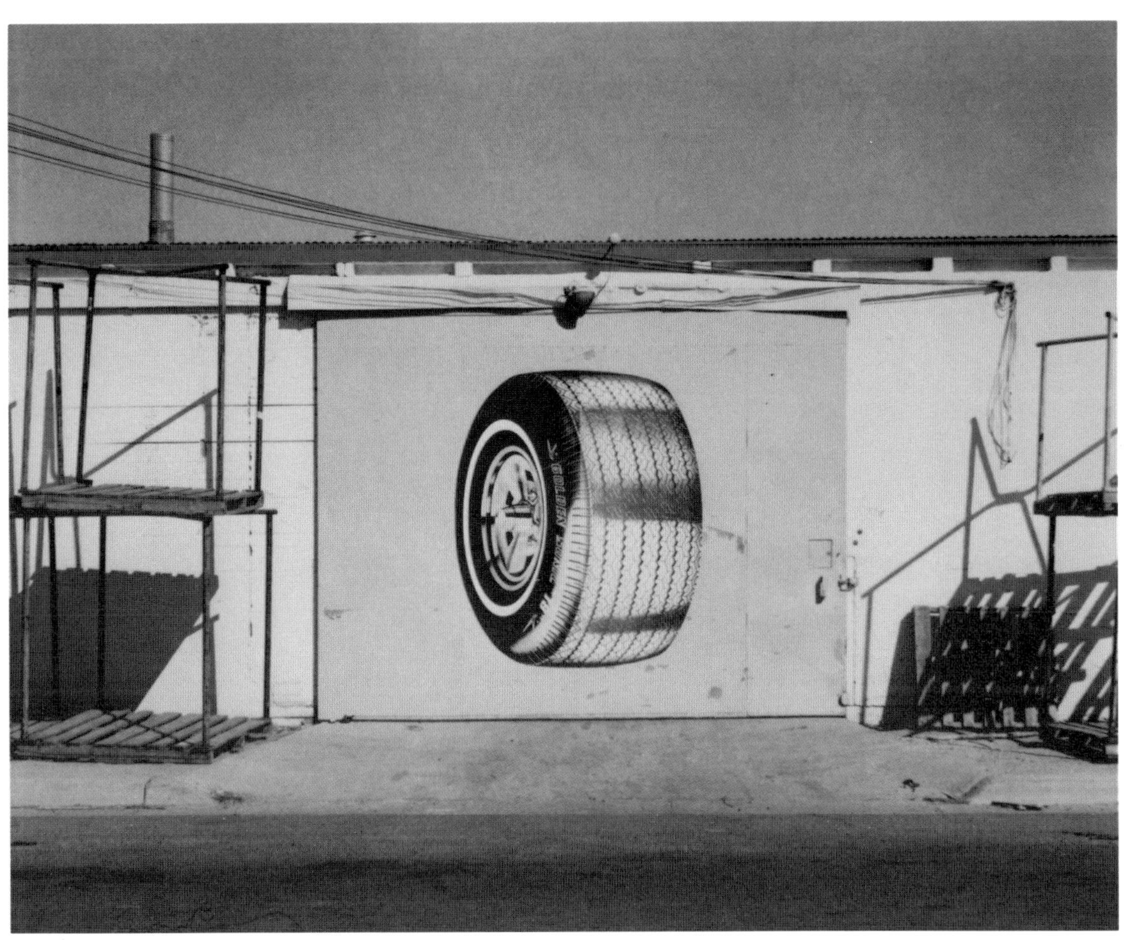

KEVIN WRIGLEY
227. Untitled, ca. 1975

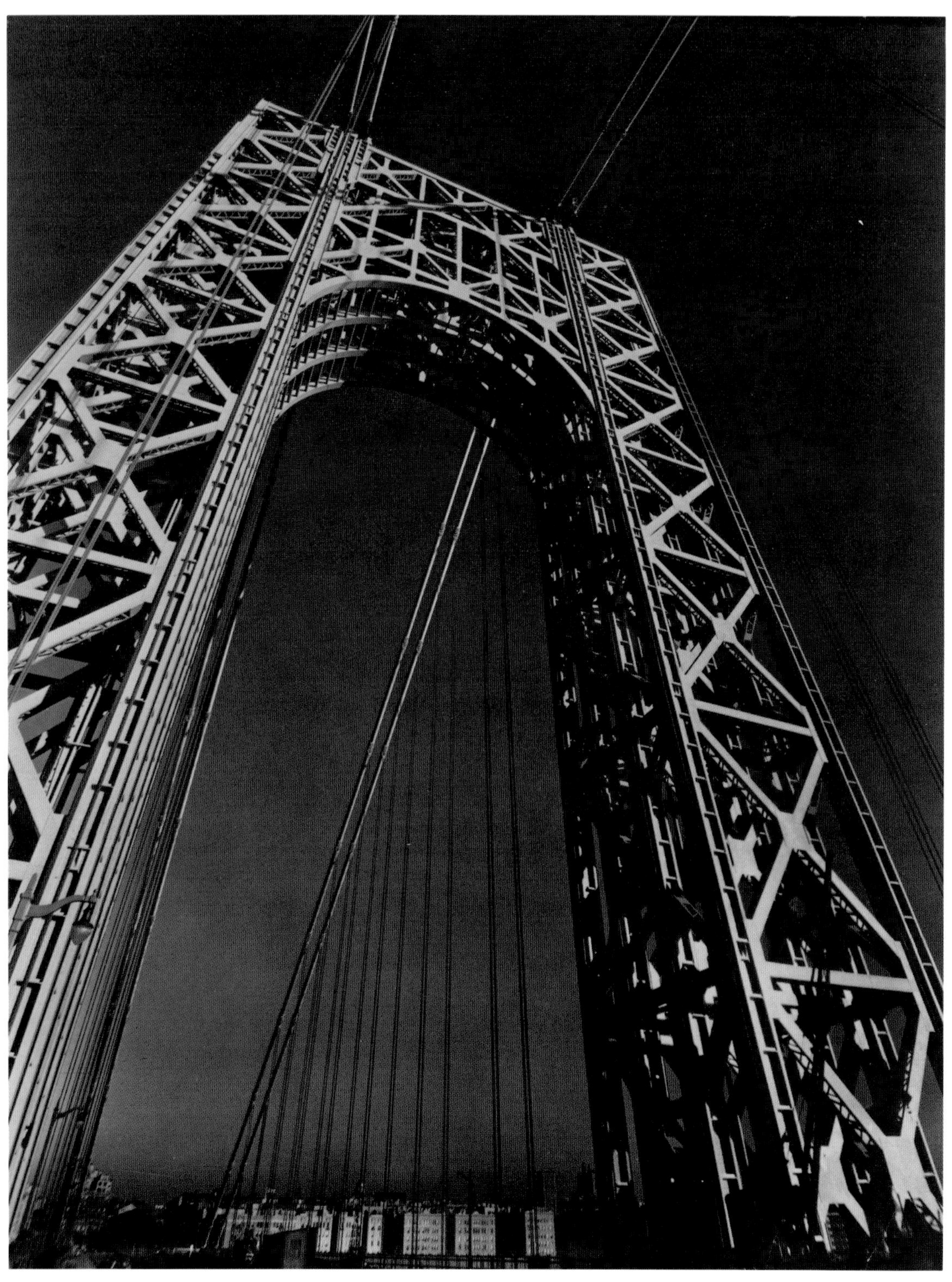

28. *The George Washington Bridge, New York*, 1931

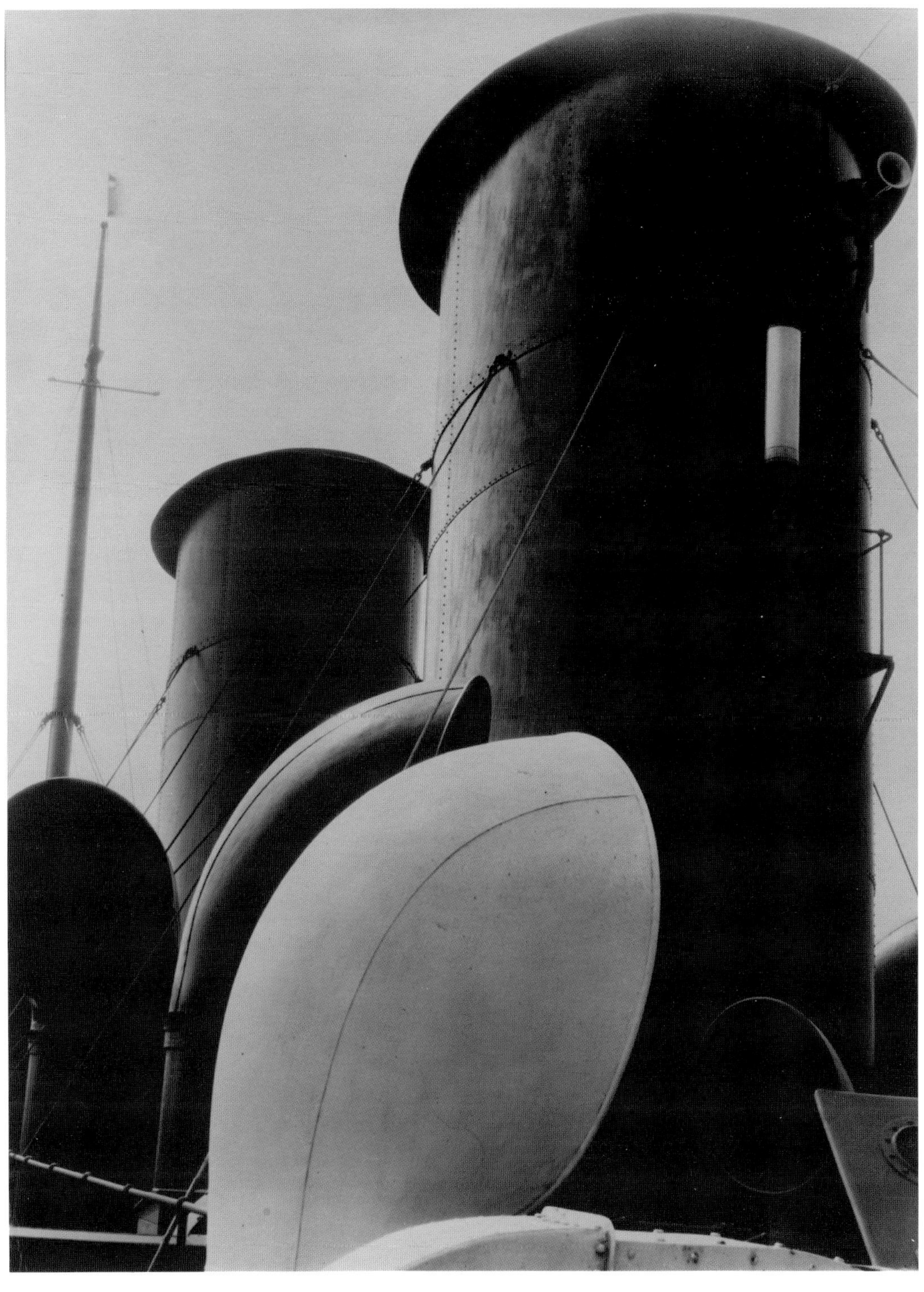

ANTON BRUEHL

5. *Liner Smoke Stacks*
(Queen Mary), 1929

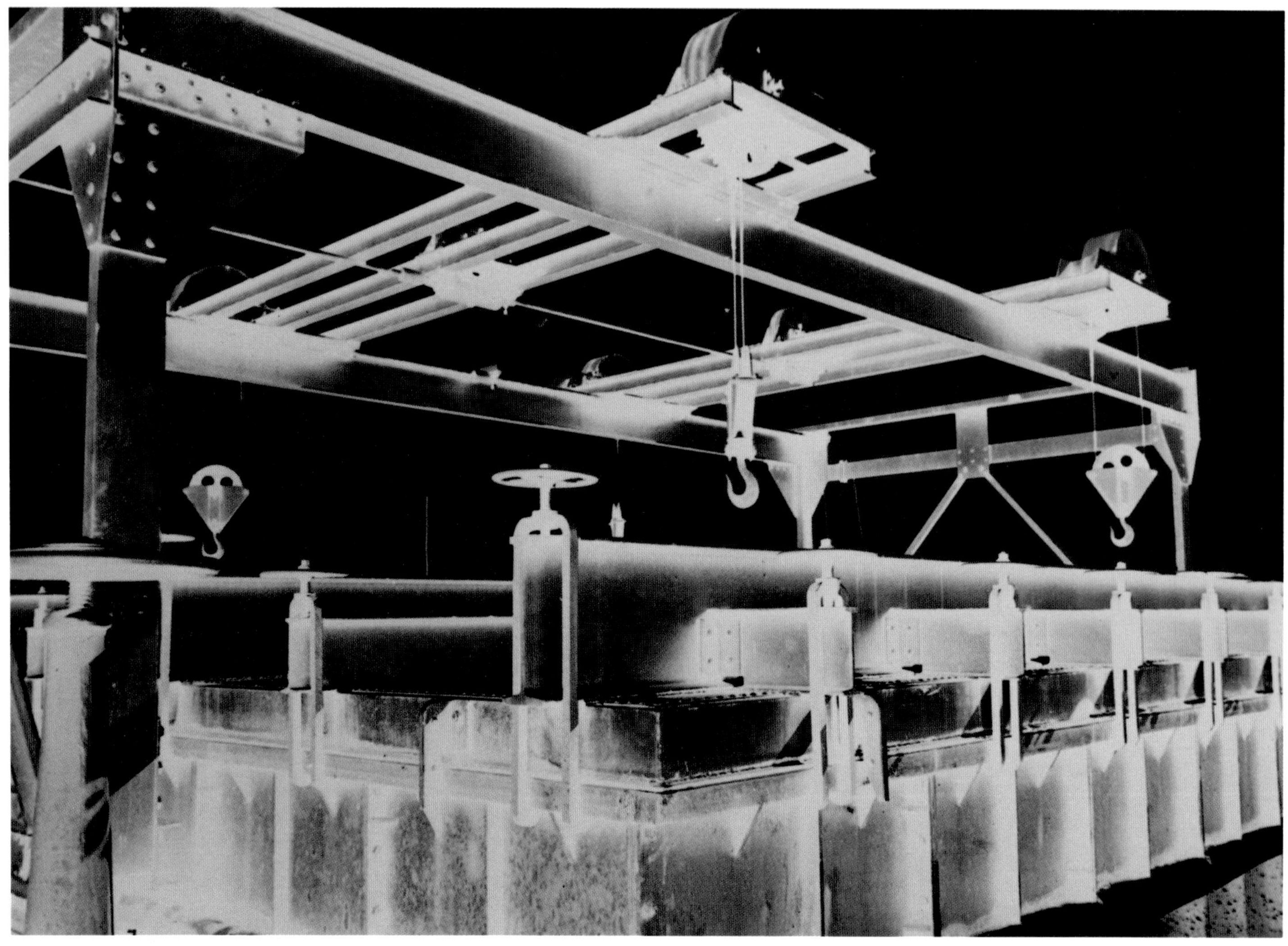

THEO BALLMER
1. Untitled, ca. 1932

BERNHARD
AND HILLA BECHER
Clockwise from top left.

214. *Kalköfen, ca. 1920,
bei Maubeuge,
Nordfrankreich (Lime Kiln,
ca. 1920, near Maubeuge,
Northern France), 1963*

*Förderturm, 1920, Fosse
"Dutemple," Valenciennes,
Nordfrankreich (Front
Tower, 1920, Fosse
"Dutemple," Valenciennes,
Northern France), 1967*

*Kühlturm, ca. 1950,
Zeche "Victoria, Mathias,"
Essen, Ruhrgebeit
(Cooling Tower, ca. 1950,
Coal Mine, "Victoria,
Mathias," Essen, Ruhr
District), 1963*

*Untitled (refinery),
ca. 1960-69*

*Wasserfurm, ca. 1920,
Liege, Belgien (Water
Tower, ca. 1920, Liege,
Belgium), 1968*

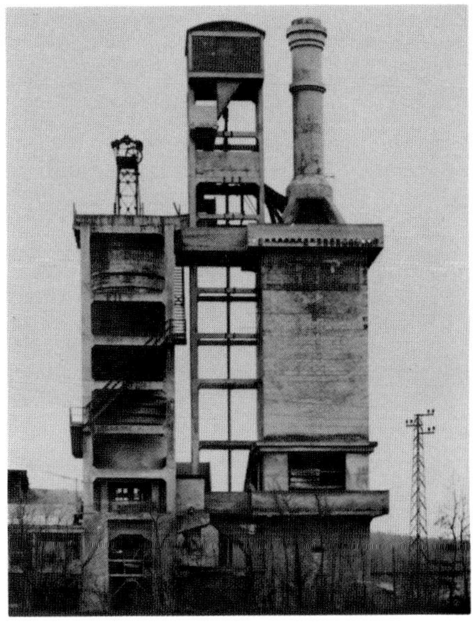

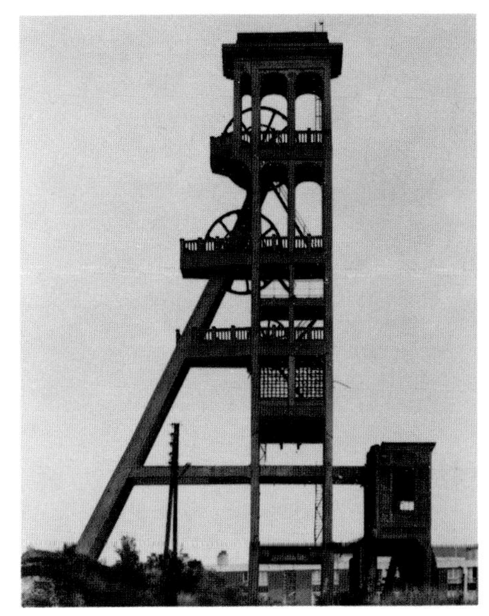

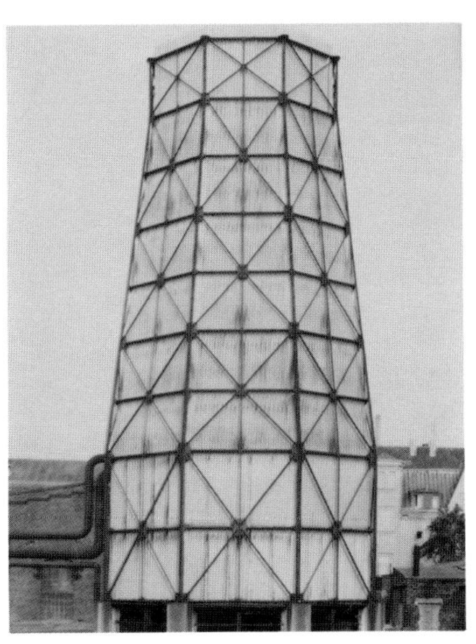

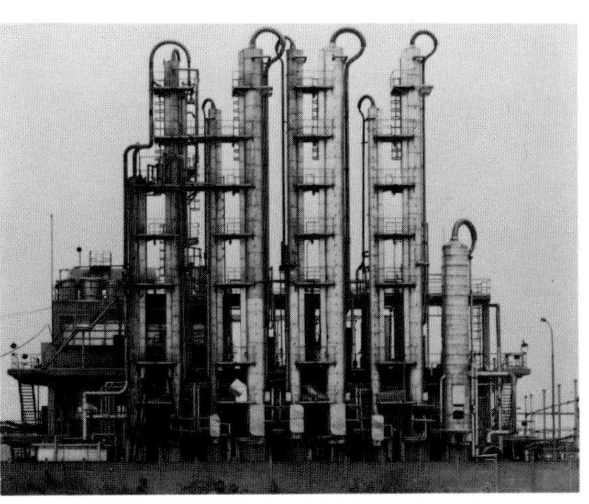

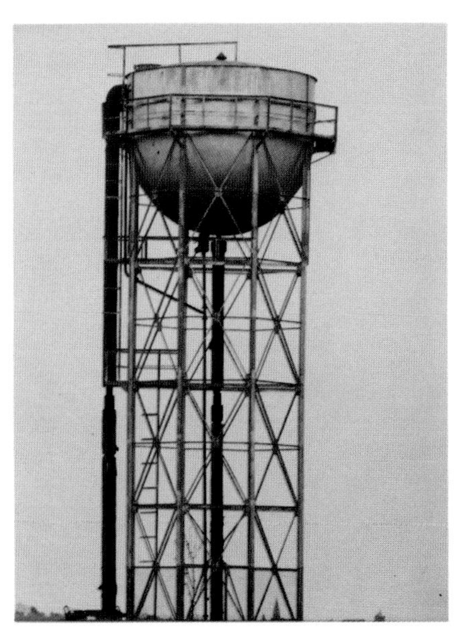

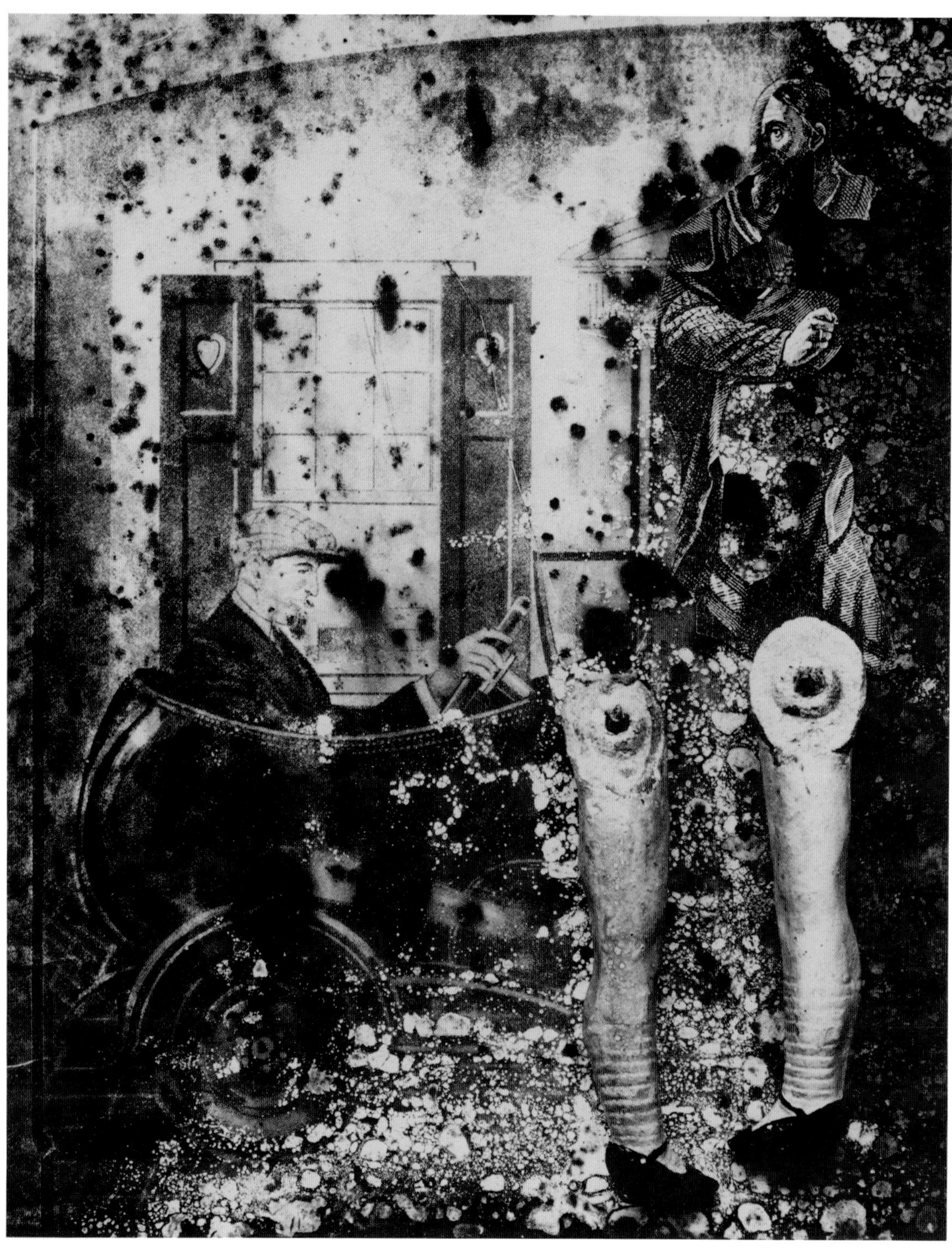

FREDERICK SOMMER
184. Untitled, 1950

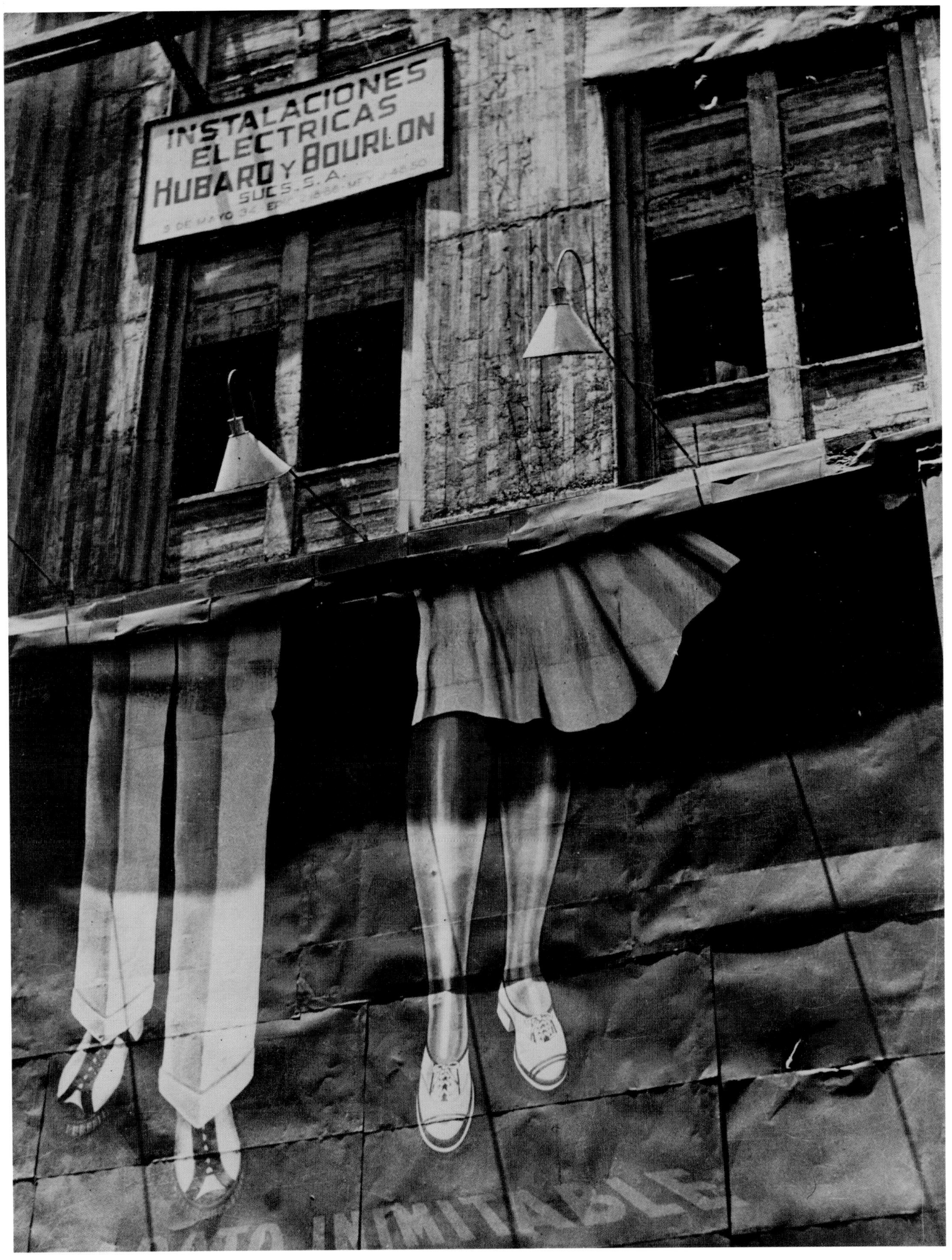

MANUEL ALVAREZ BRAVO
40. *Dos Pares de Piernas*
(Two Pairs of Legs),
1928-29/1977

RALPH EUGENE MEATYARD
164. Untitled, ca. 1960

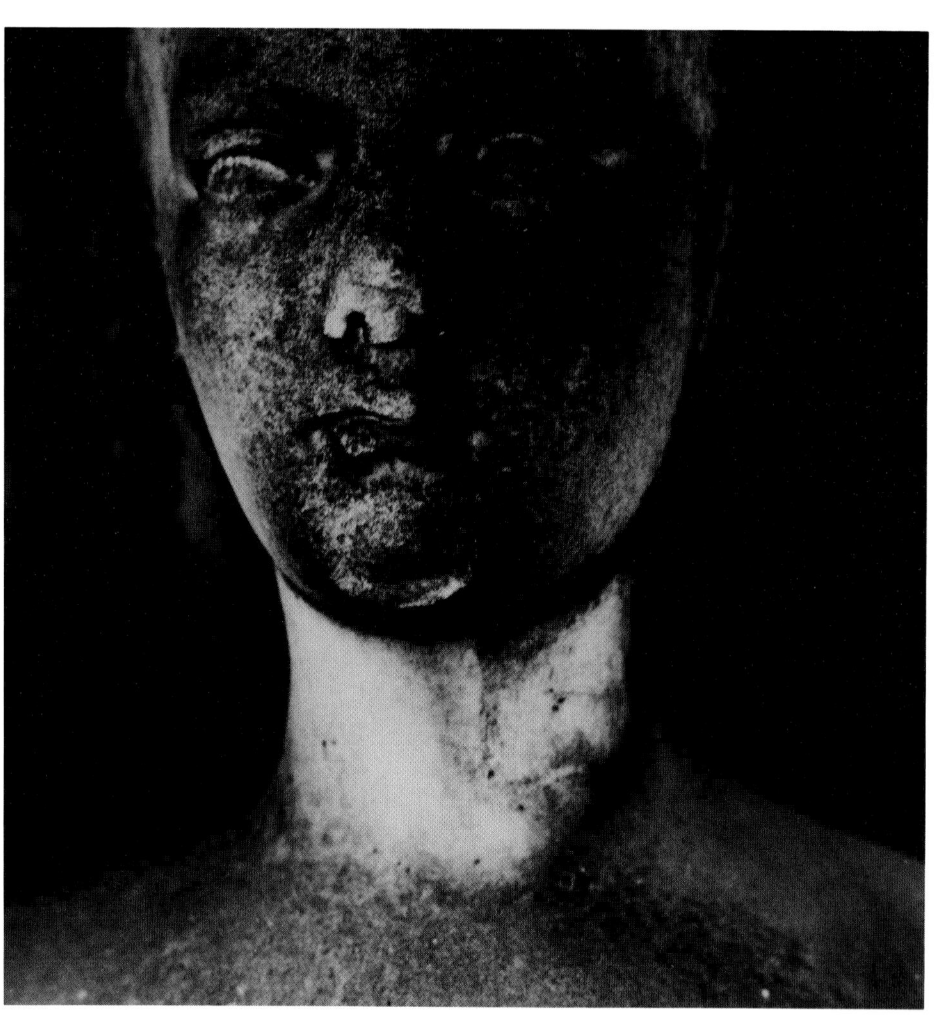

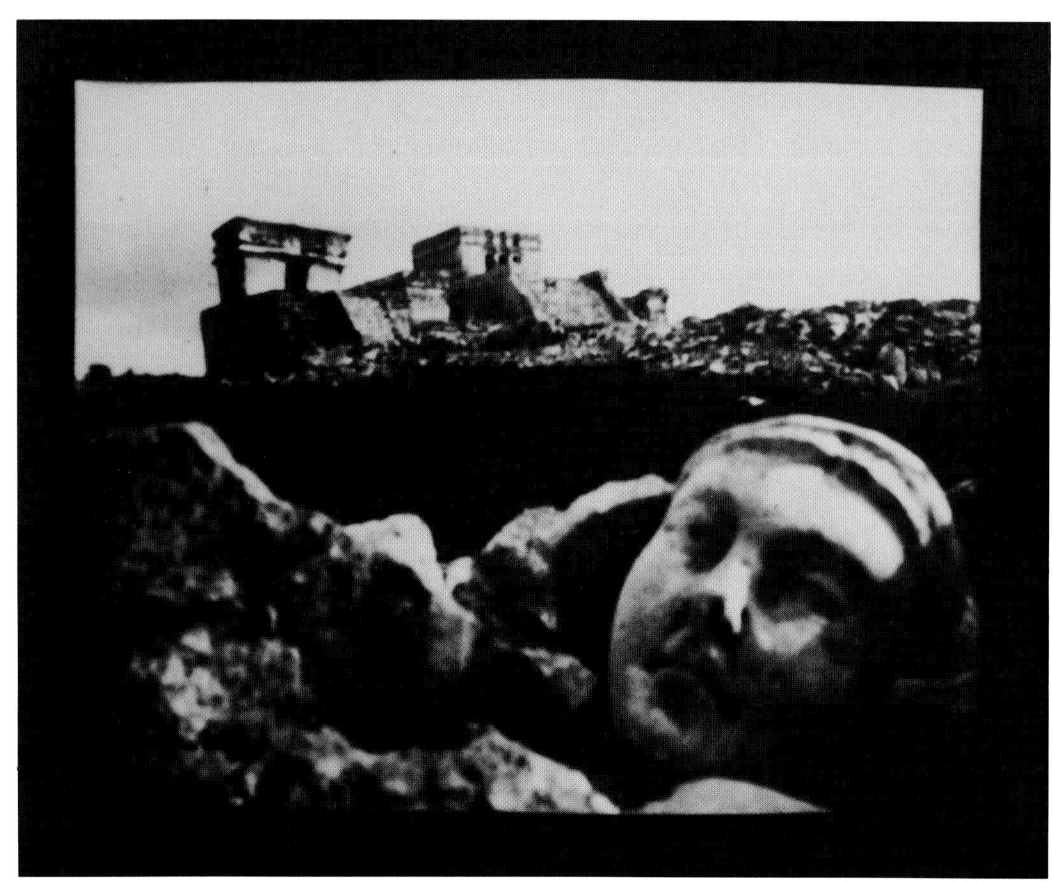

RUTH THORNE-THOMSEN
195. Untitled, 1979

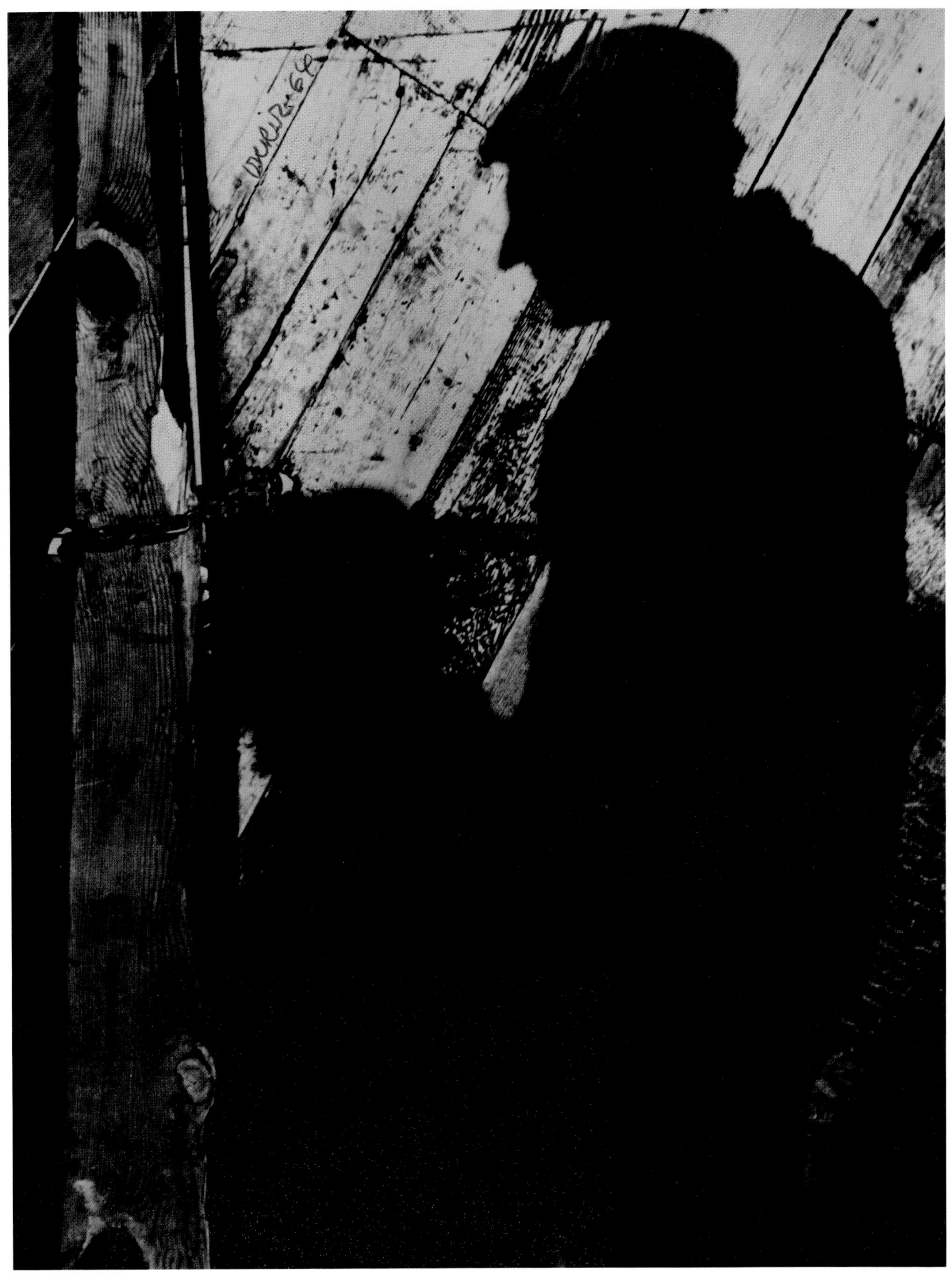

VILEM KRIZ
153. *Berkeley, 1964*

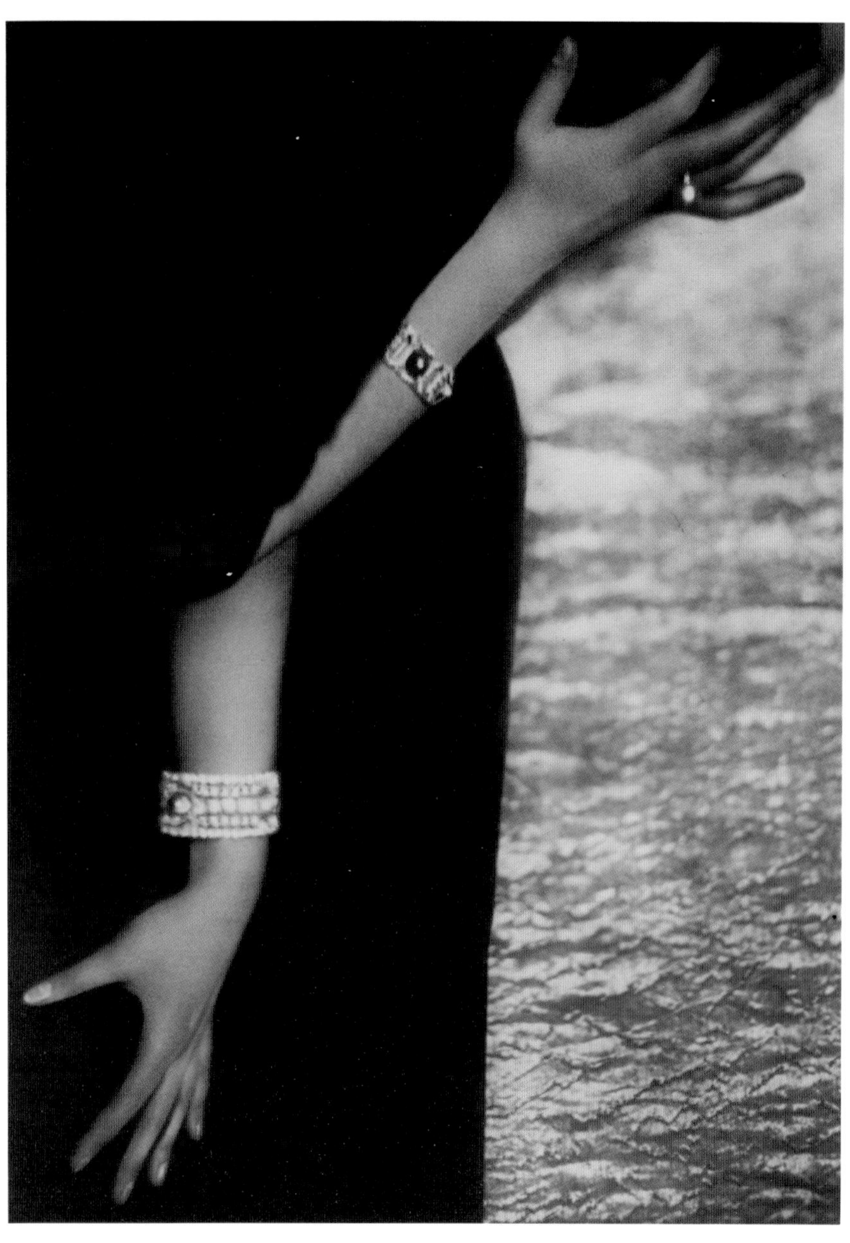

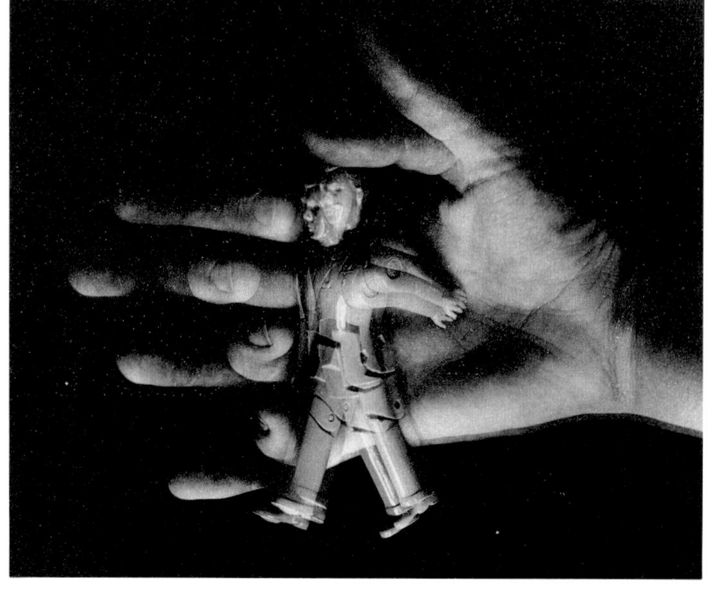

JERRY N. UELSMANN
197. *Fleeing Man*, 1961

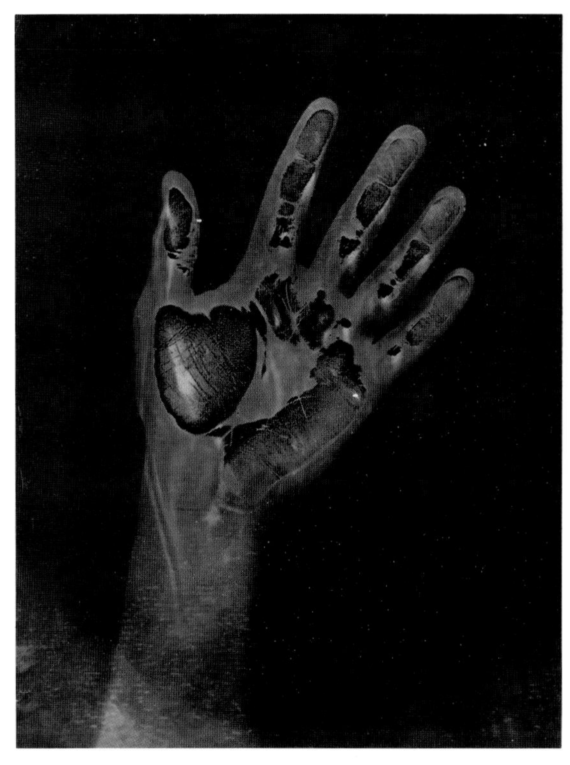

VAL TELBERG
189. *My Hand,* ca. 1950-53

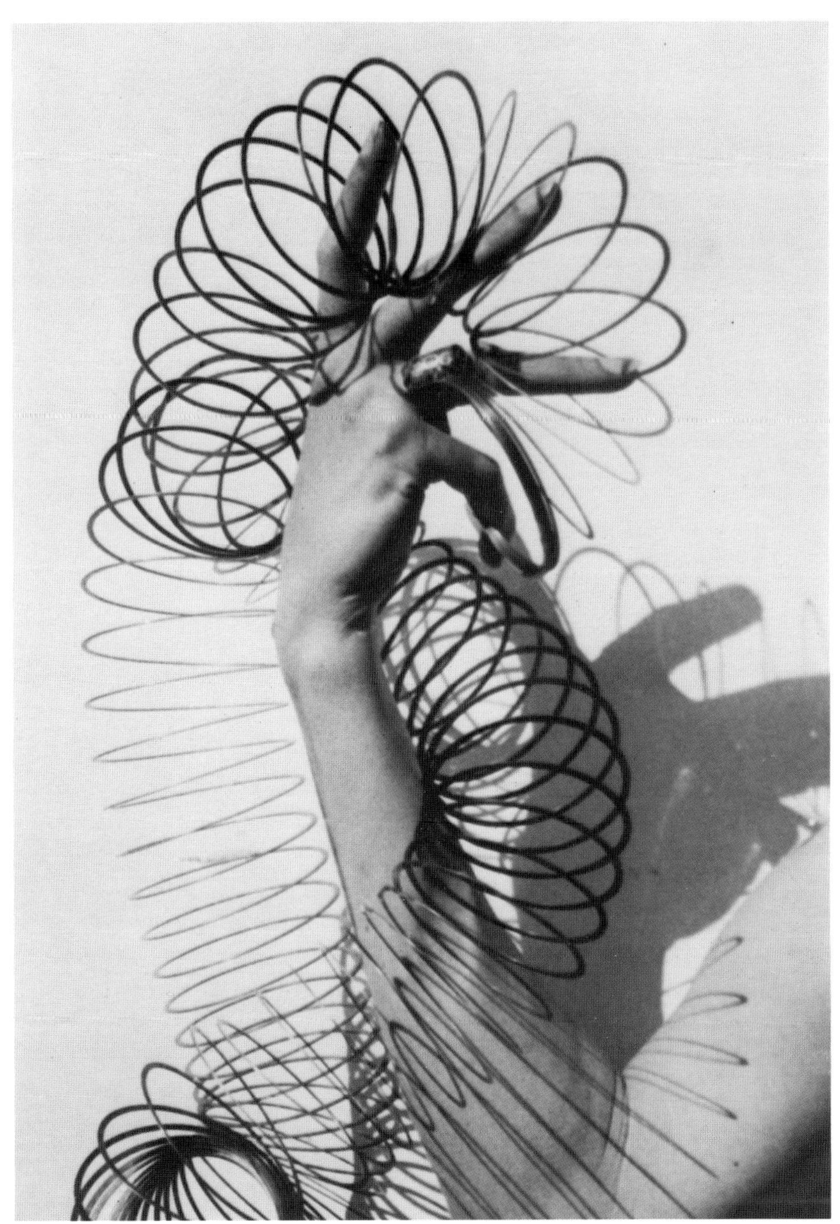

HENRY SWIFT
104. Untitled, 1930s

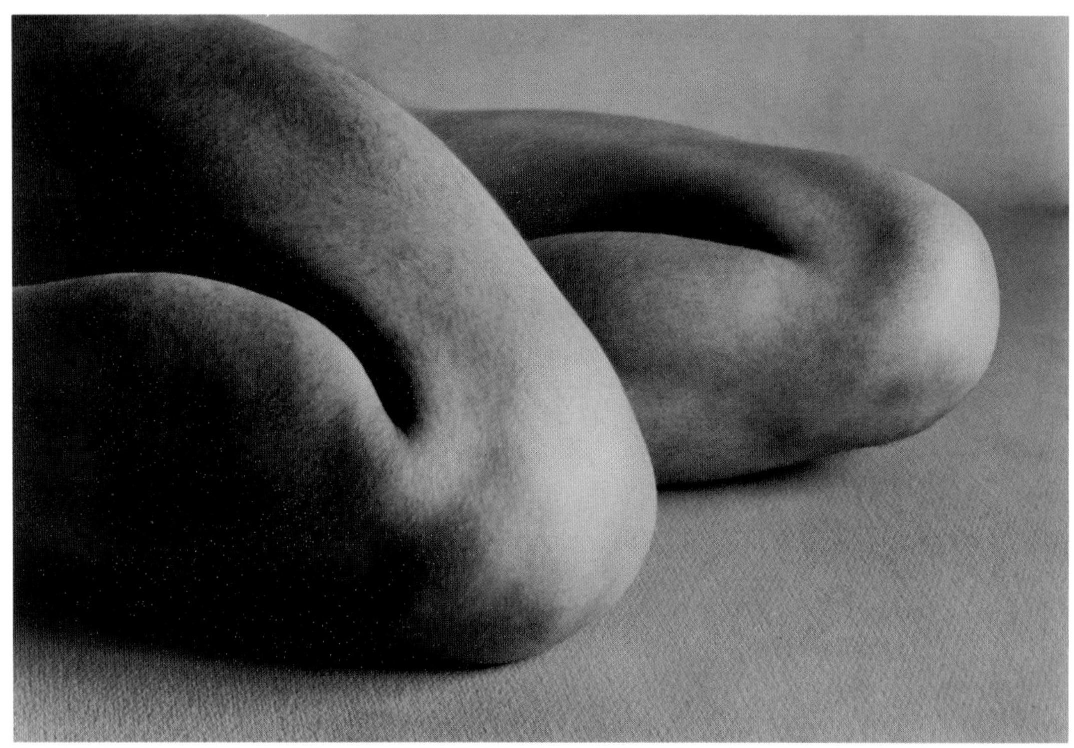

EDWARD WESTON
112. *Knees,* 1927

© 1981 Arizona Board of
Regents, Center for Creative
Photography

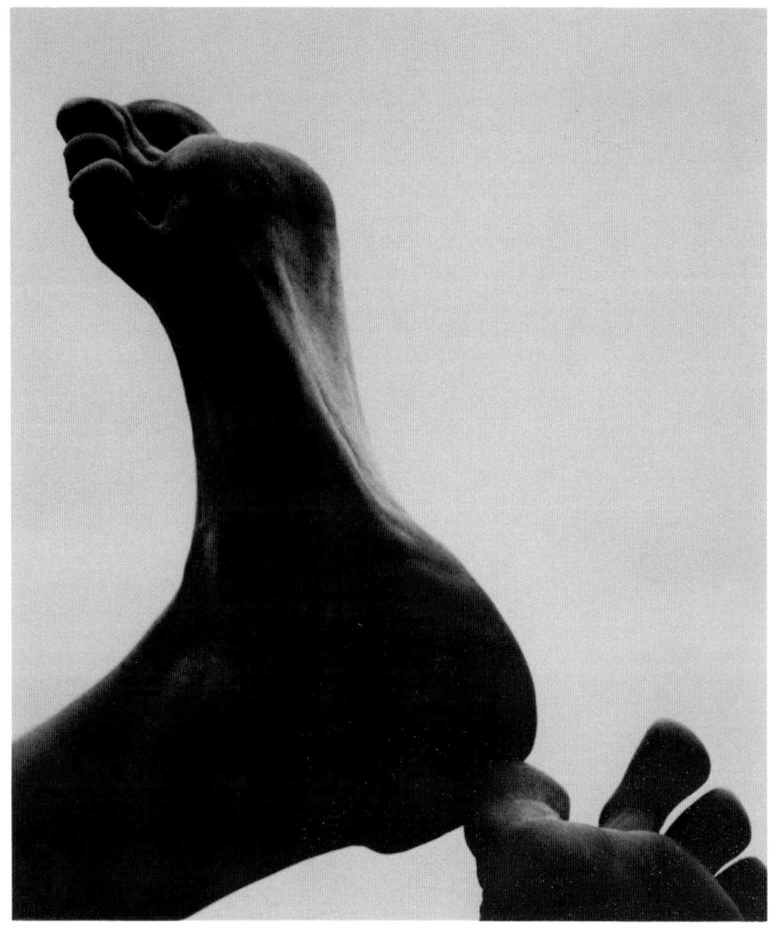

AARON SISKIND
181. *Feet,* 1957

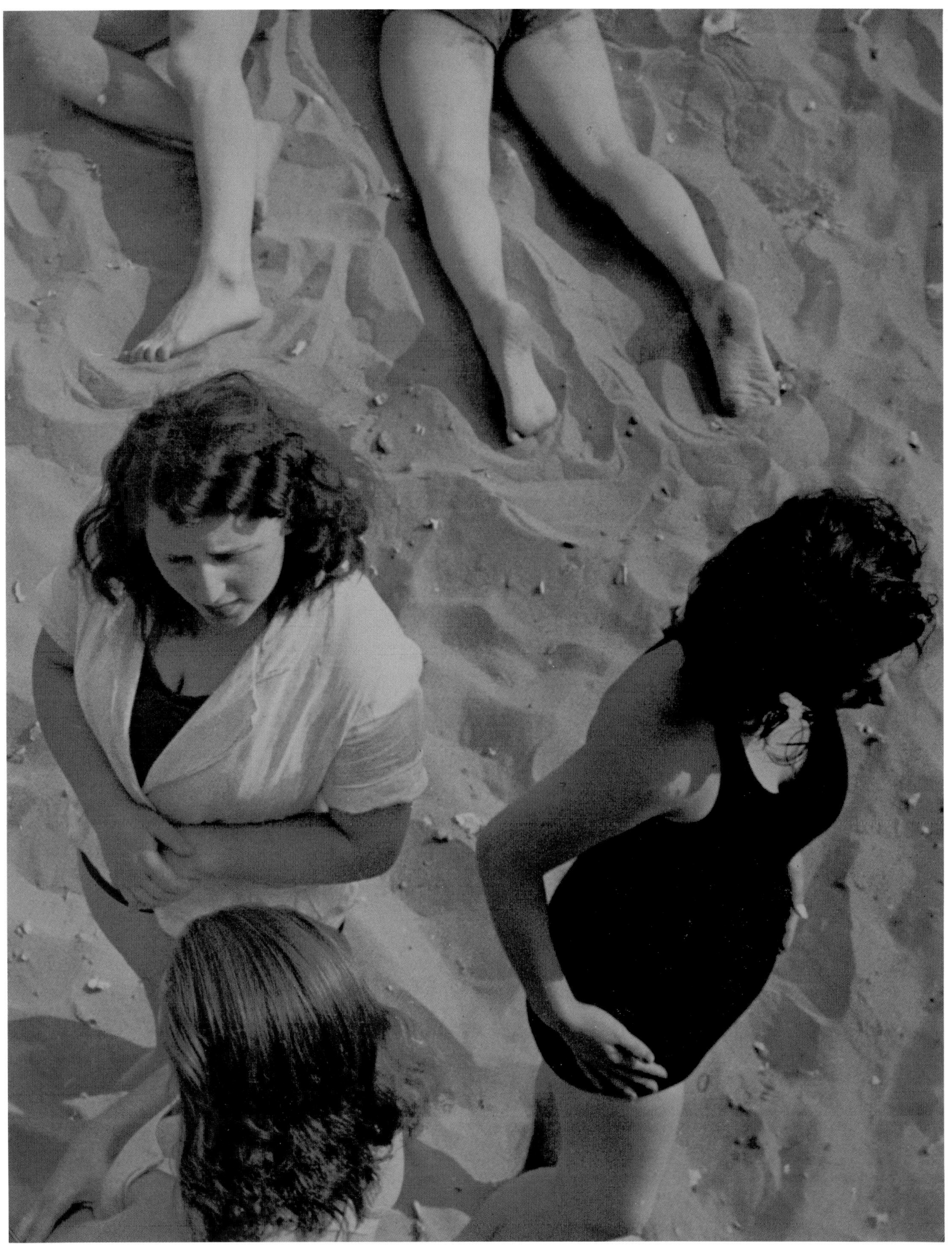

YASUO KUNIYOSHI
78. *Coney Island*, 1938

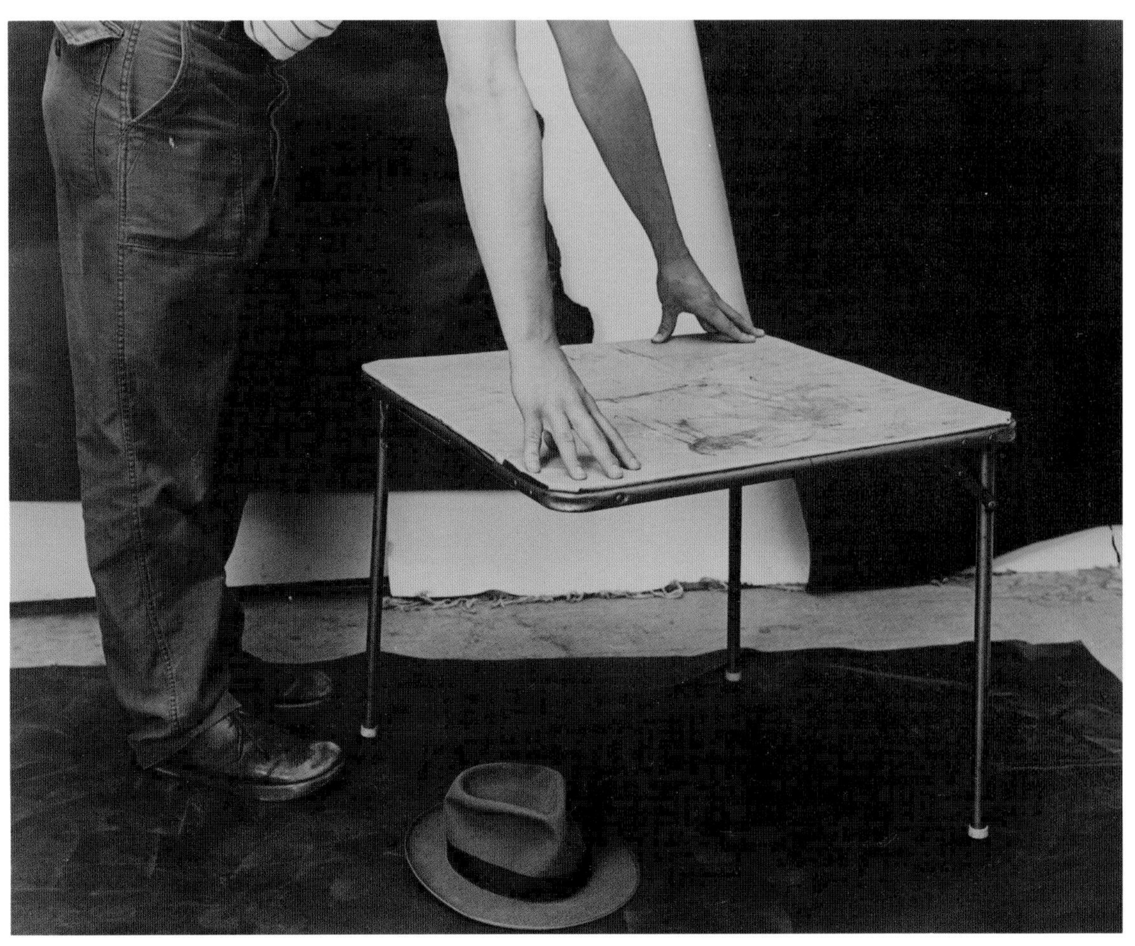

PHILLIP GALGIANI
140. *3 Legged Table, 1977/1978*

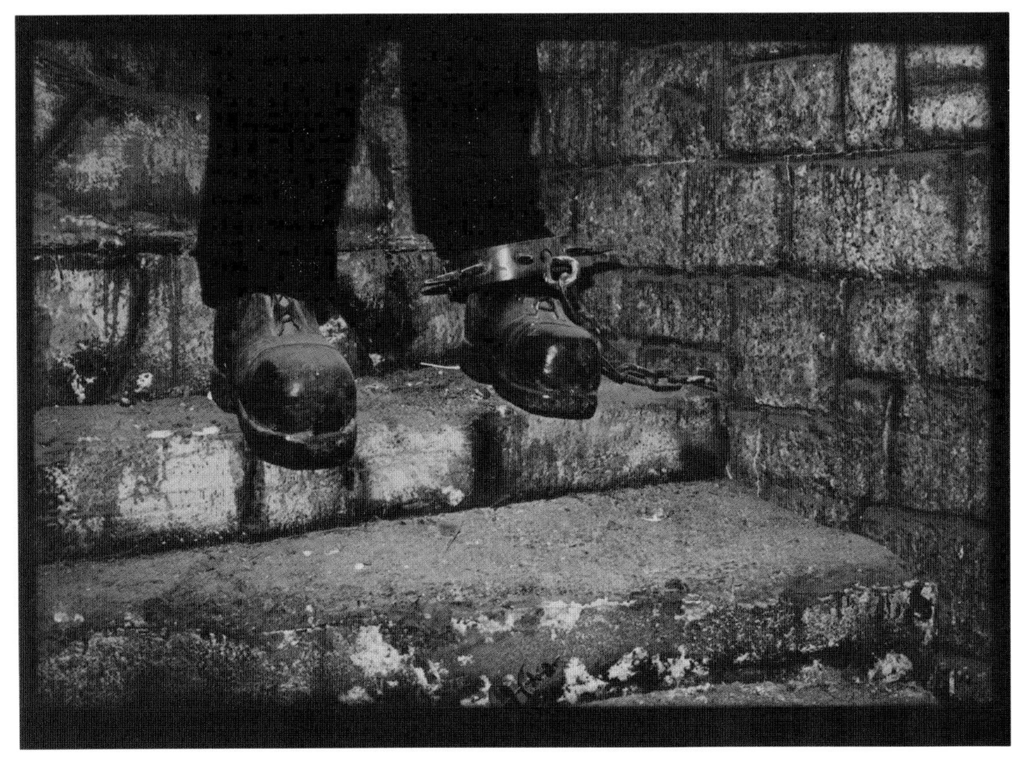

NEAL WHITE
204. *San Francisco, 1978*

JOSEPH D. JACHNA
149. *Dowdy Lake, Colorado
(Ginny's Feet), 1974*

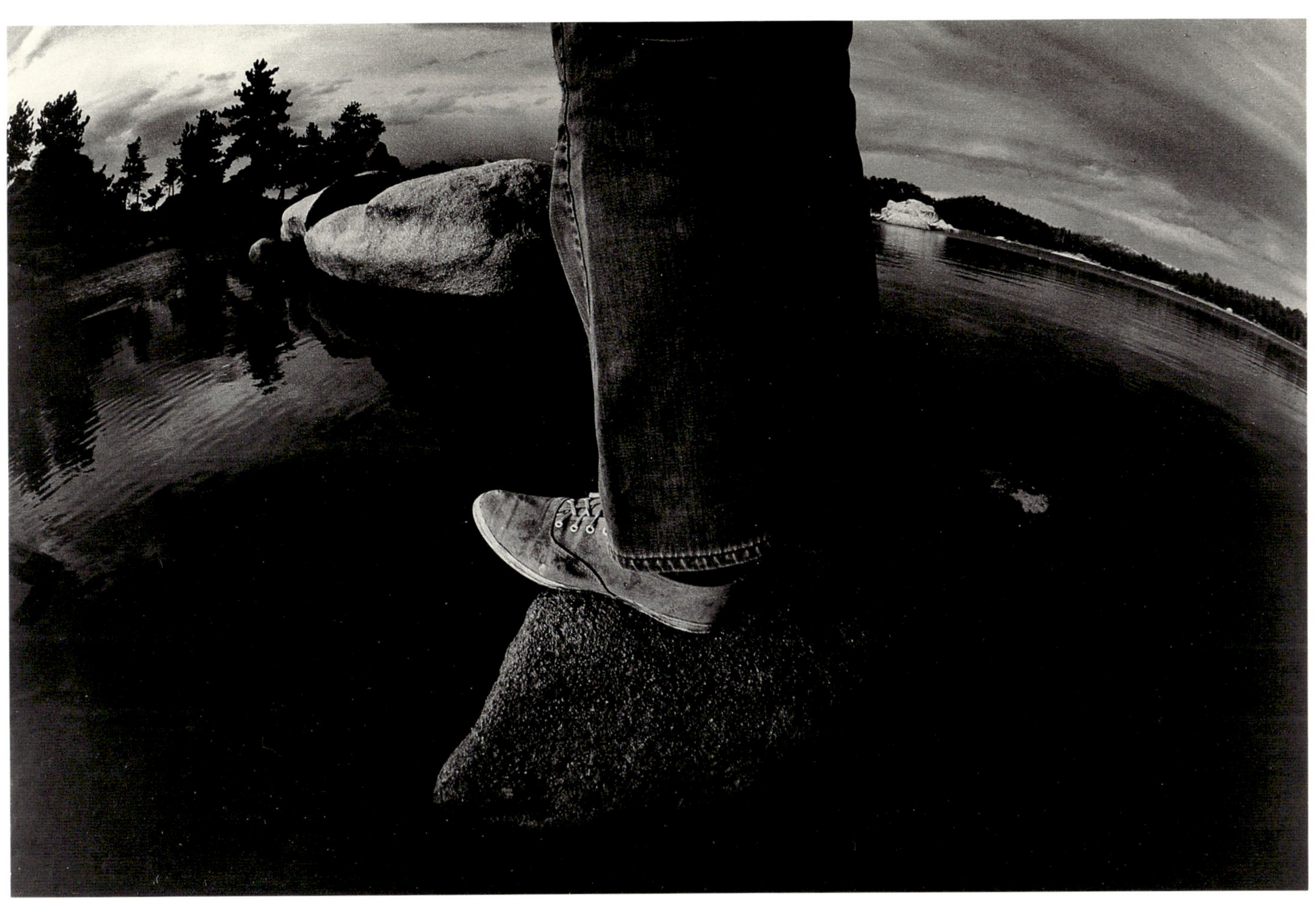

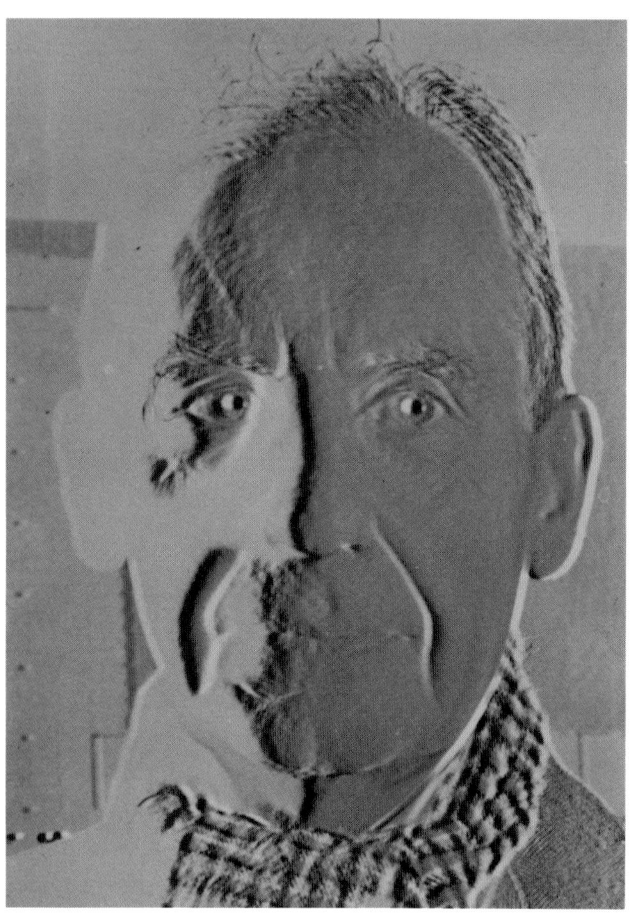

XANTI (ALEXANDER) SCHAWINSKY
175. Untitled (portrait of
Walter Gropius), 1943

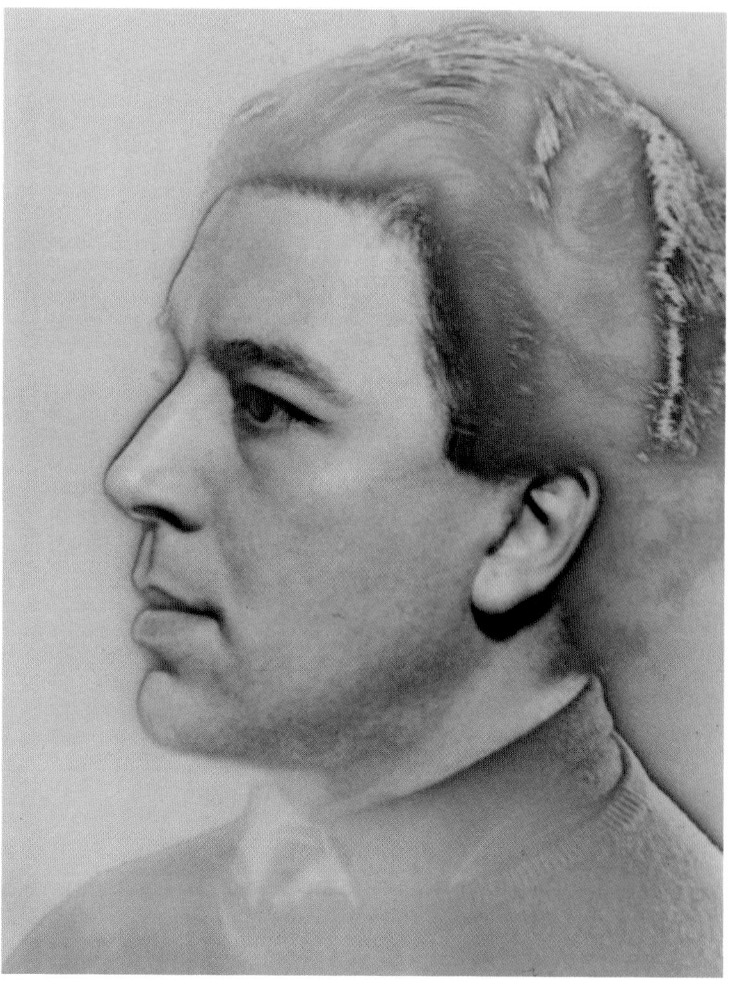

MAN RAY
86. André Breton, ca. 1930

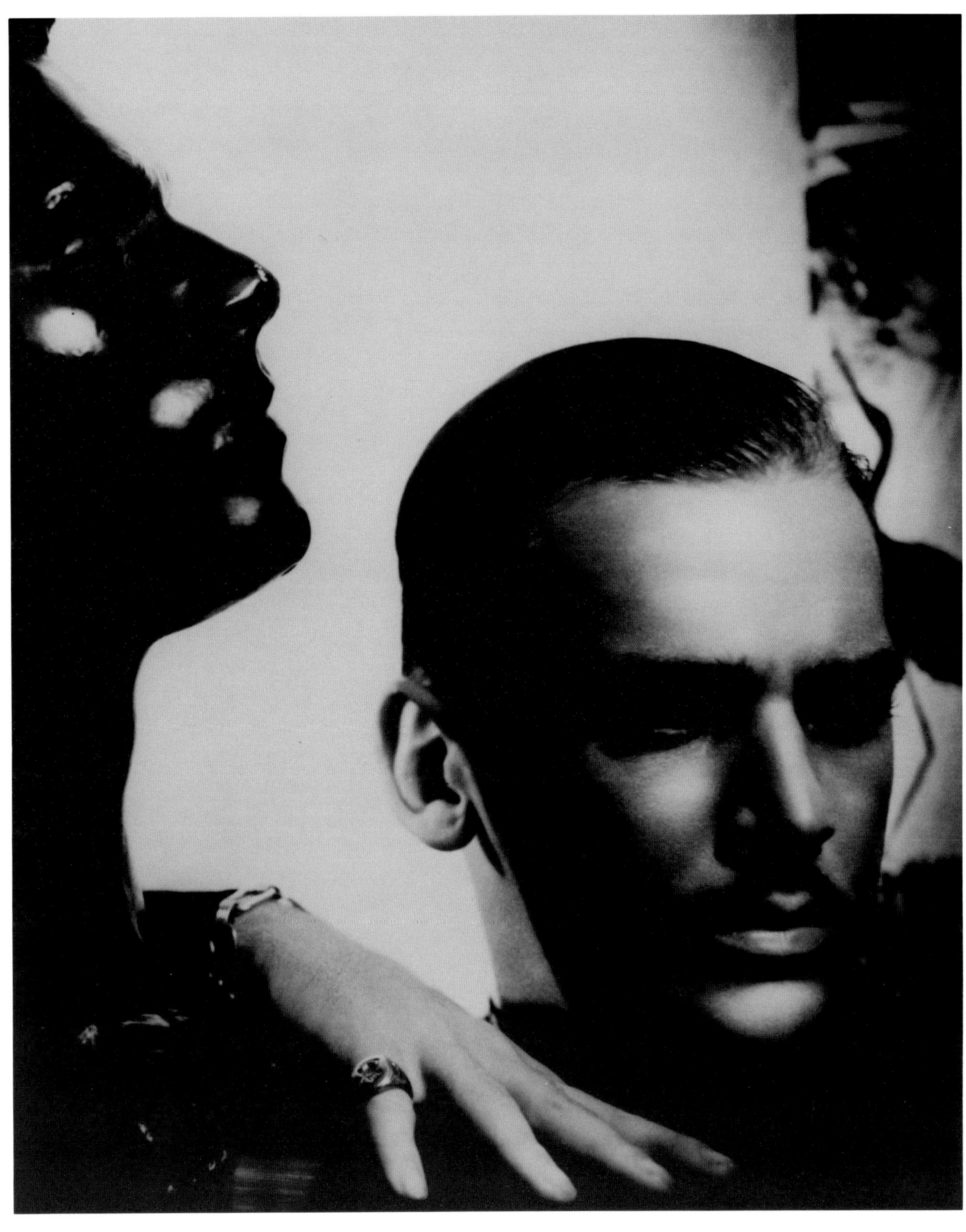

GEORGE HURRELL
66. *Douglas Fairbanks,*
ca. 1930-33/ ca. 1980

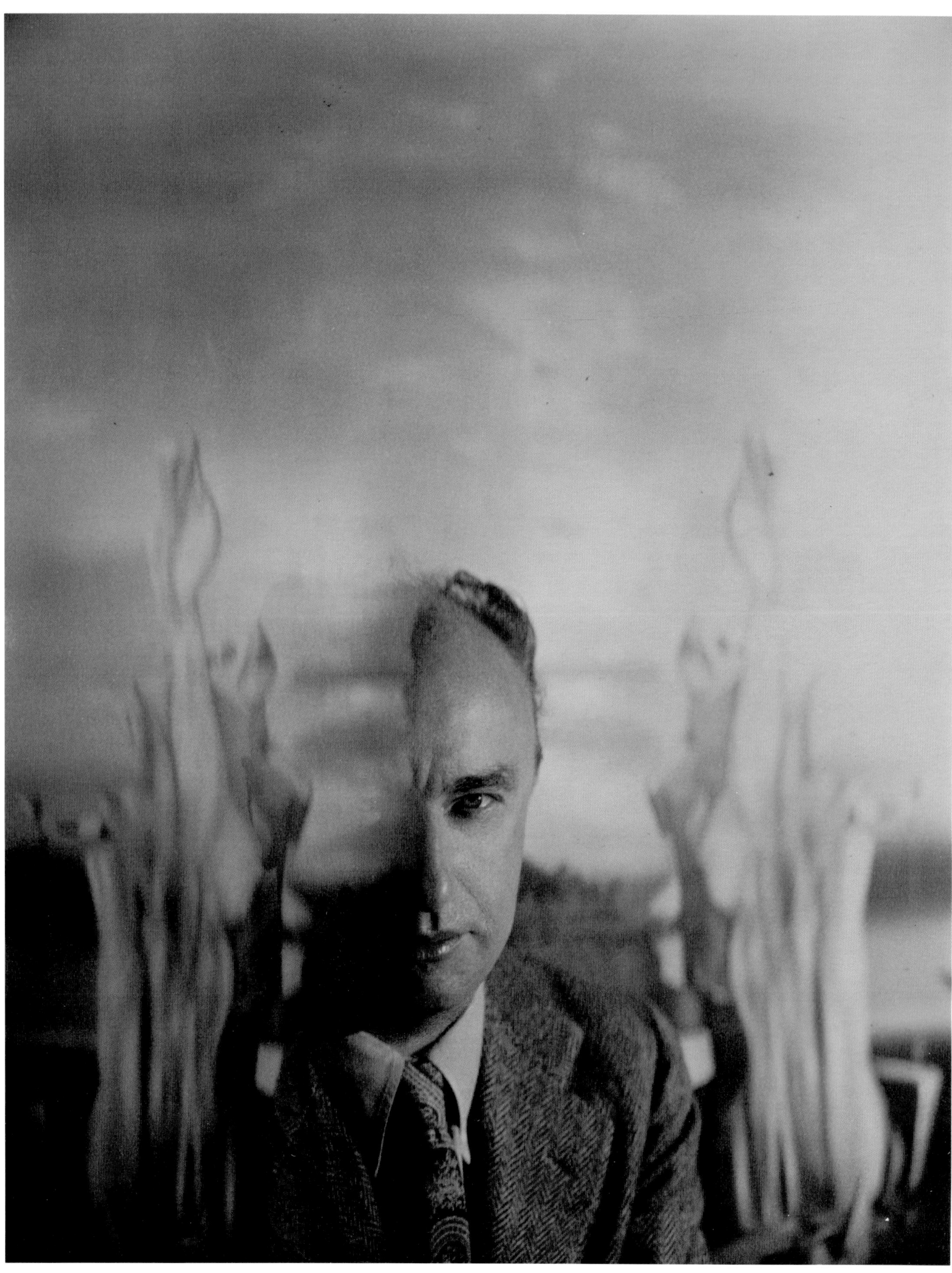

GEORGE PLATT LYNES
84. *Yves Tanguy*, ca. 1938

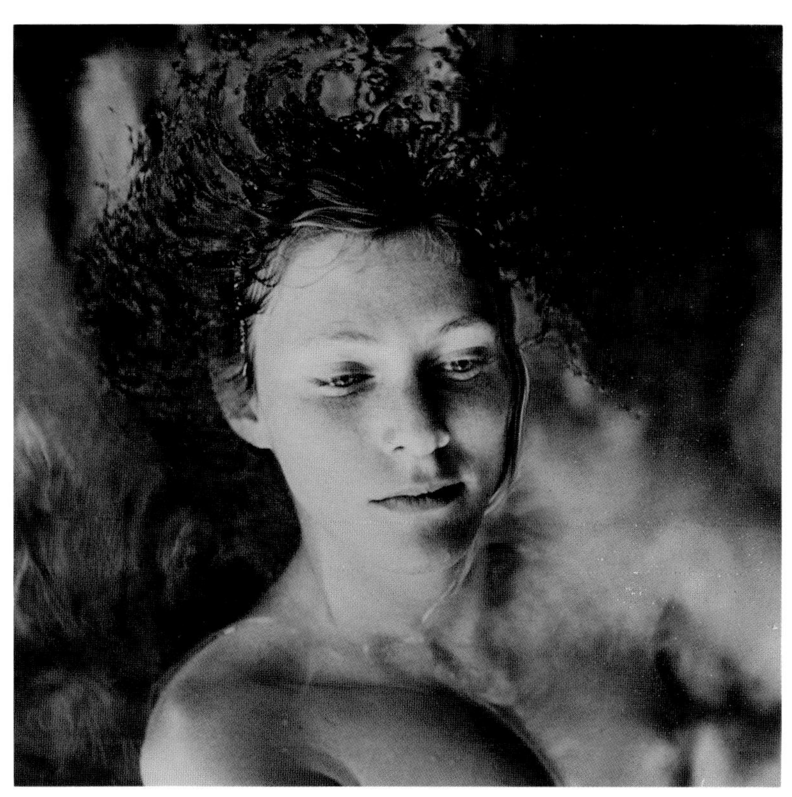

LARRY SULTAN
186. Untitled, 1972

PIERRE BOUCHER
52. Ondine, 1938

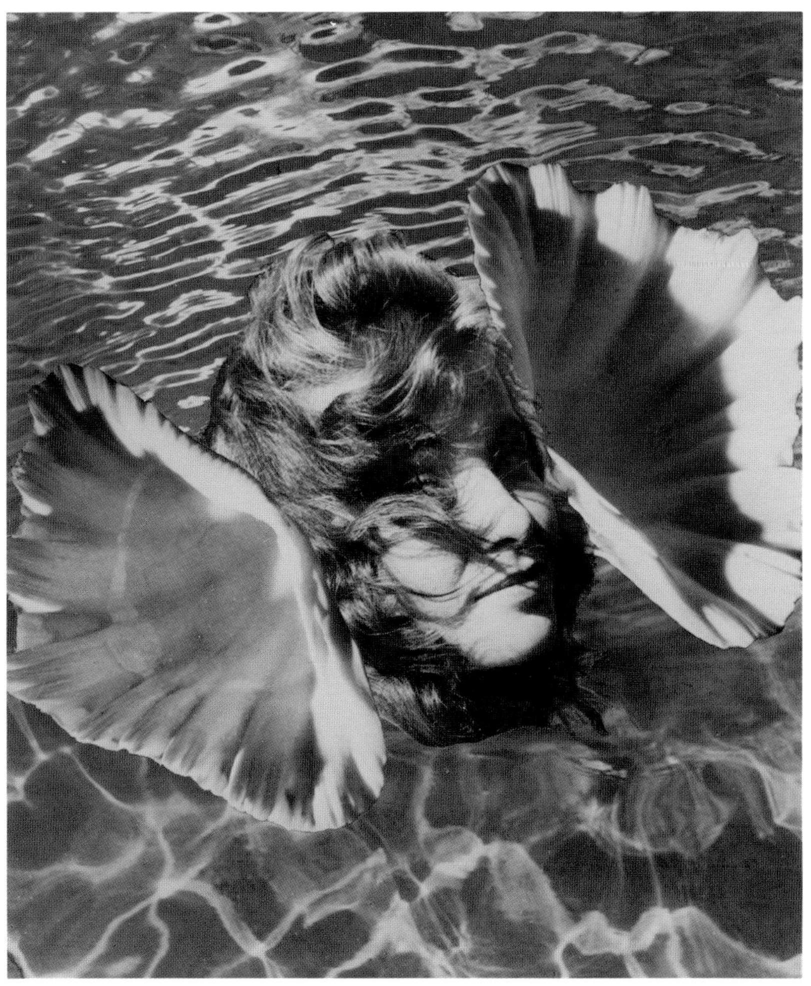

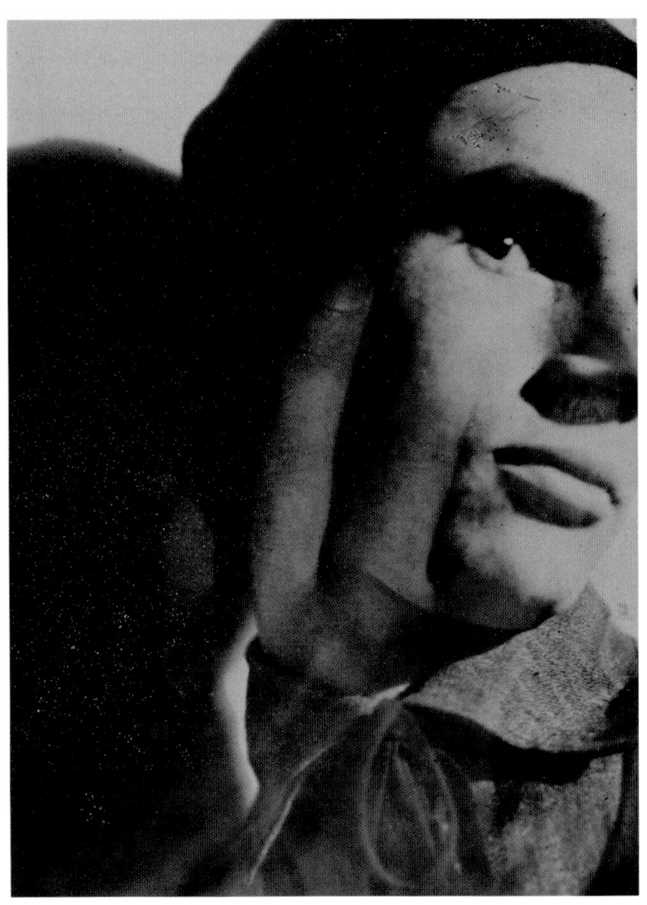

WERNER DAVID FEIST
64. Untitled (M. (?) Bahelfer),
1929

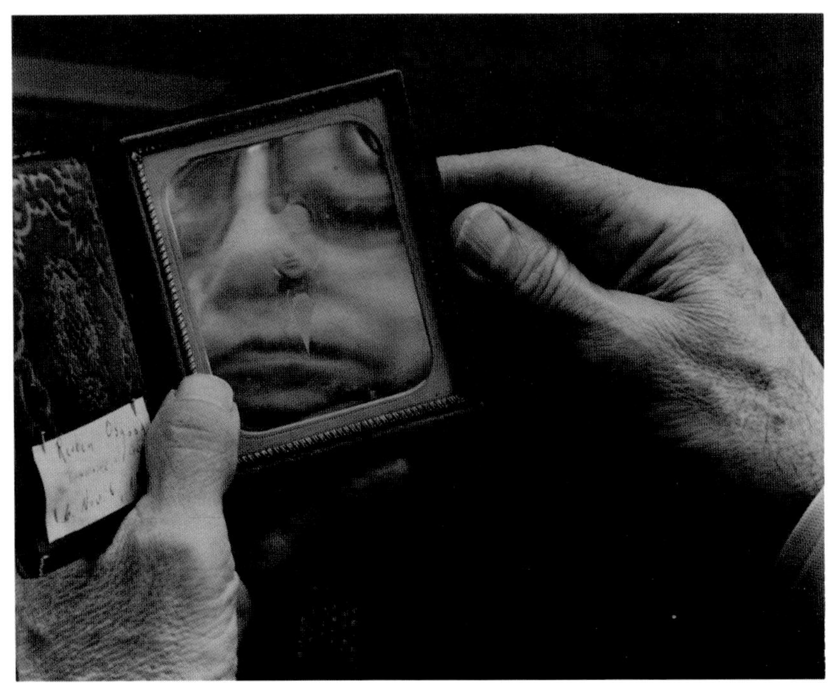

CHARLES OSGOOD
172. Untitled, 1976

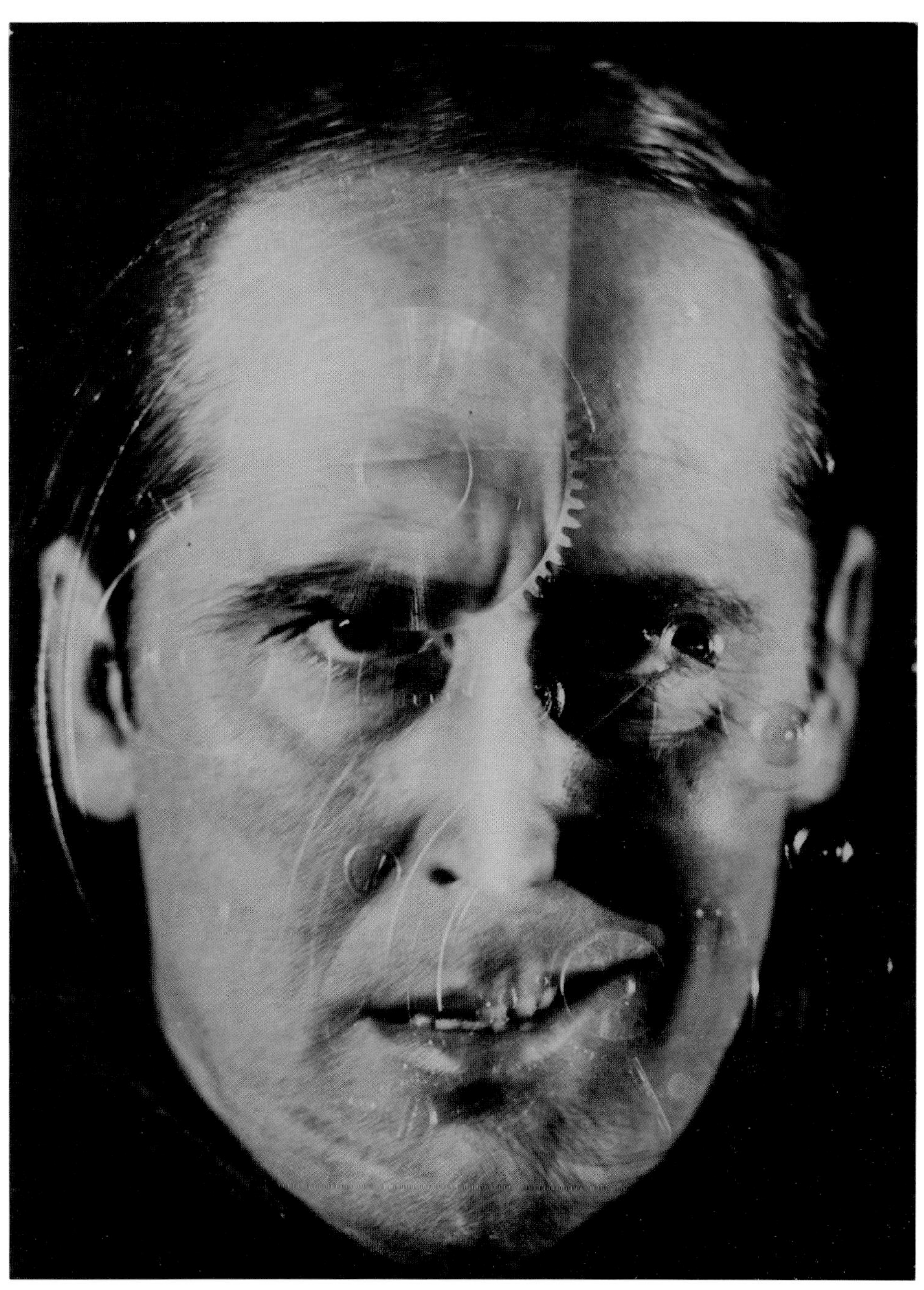

TATO (Guglielmo Sansoni)
107. *Ritratto Meccanico
di Remo Chiti (Mechanical
Portrait of Remo Chiti),*
1930

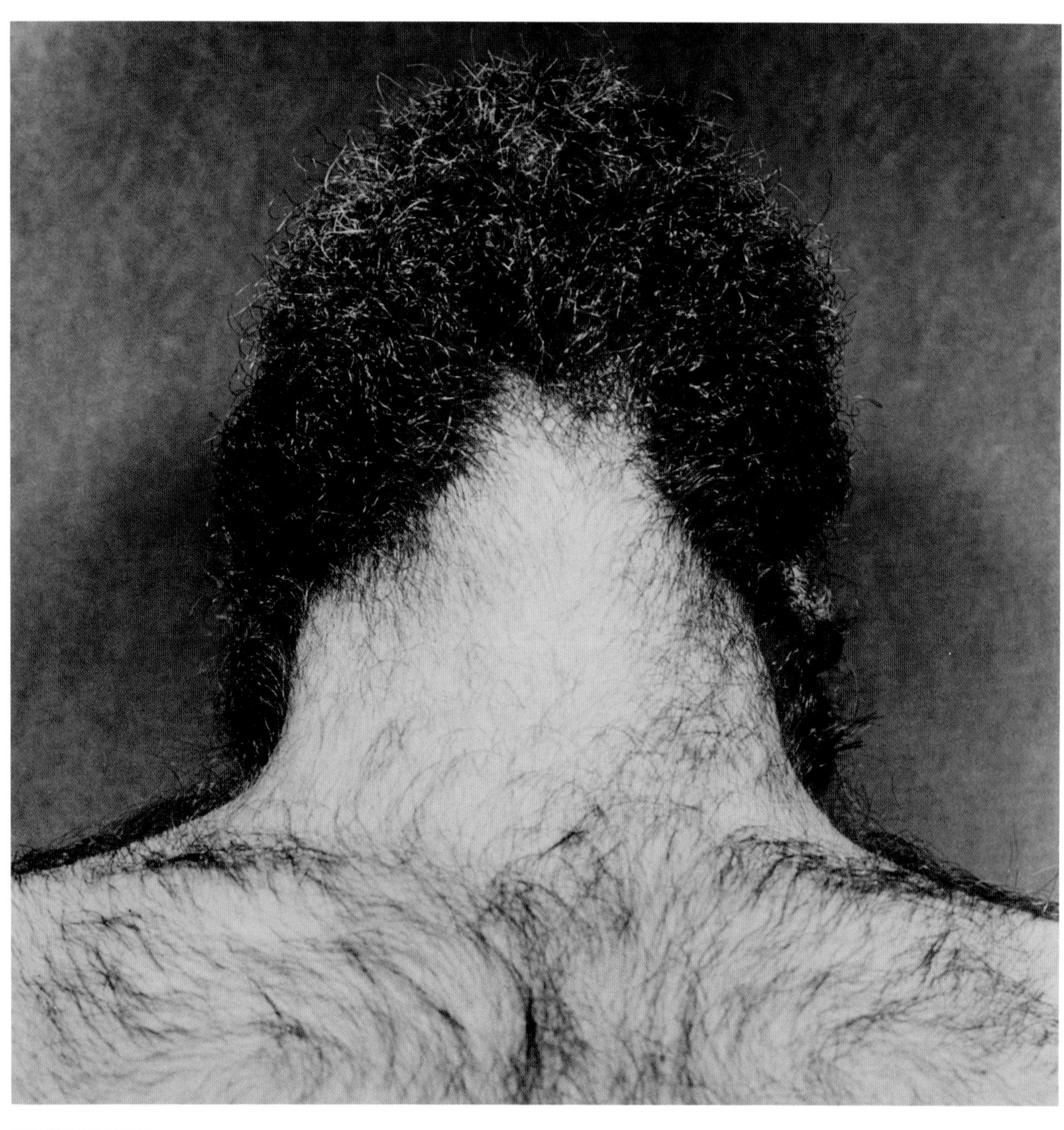

BRUCE PATTERSON
173. *Richard Burks*, 1976

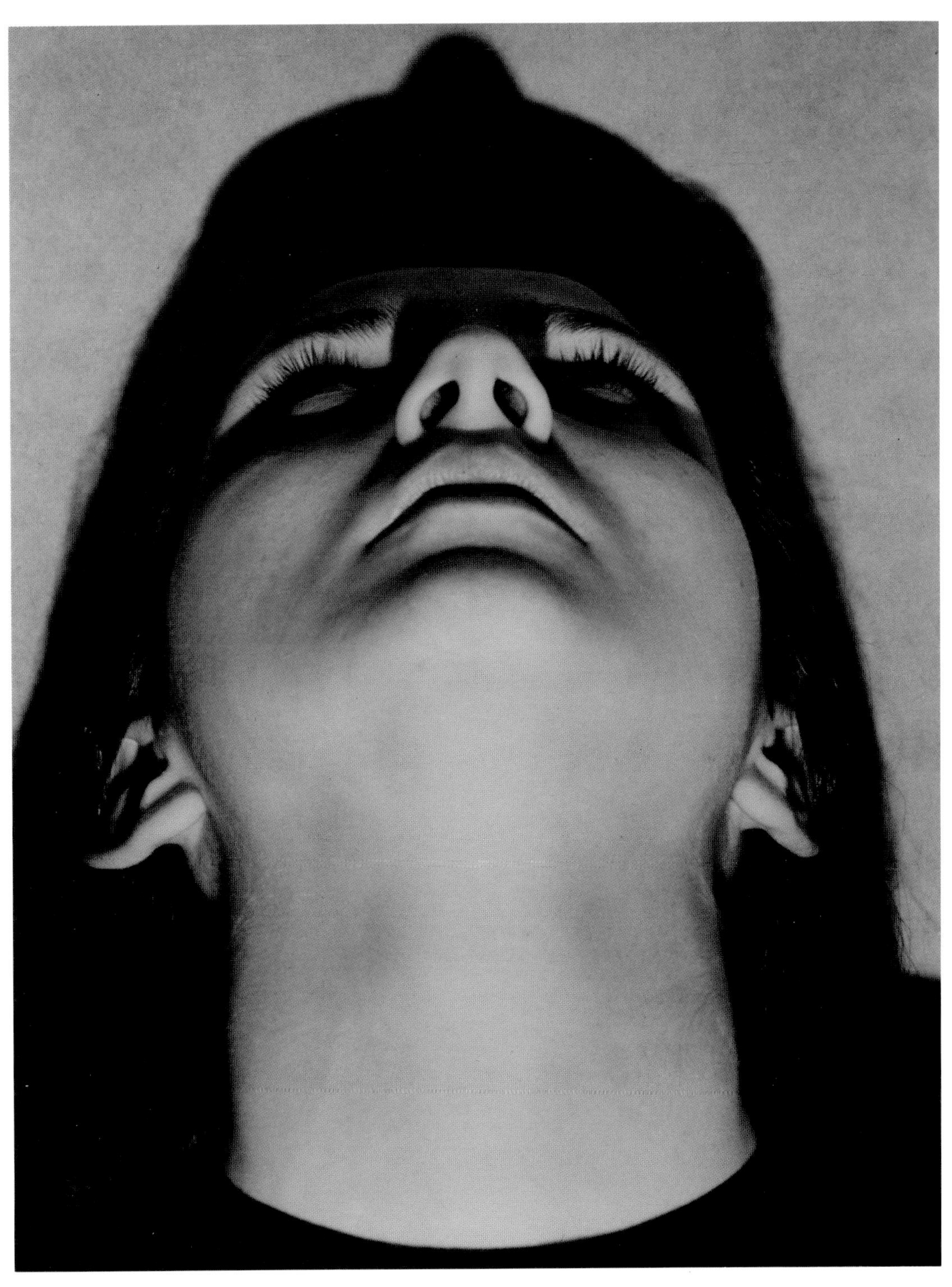

ERWIN BLUMENFELD
49. Untitled, 1937/ later print

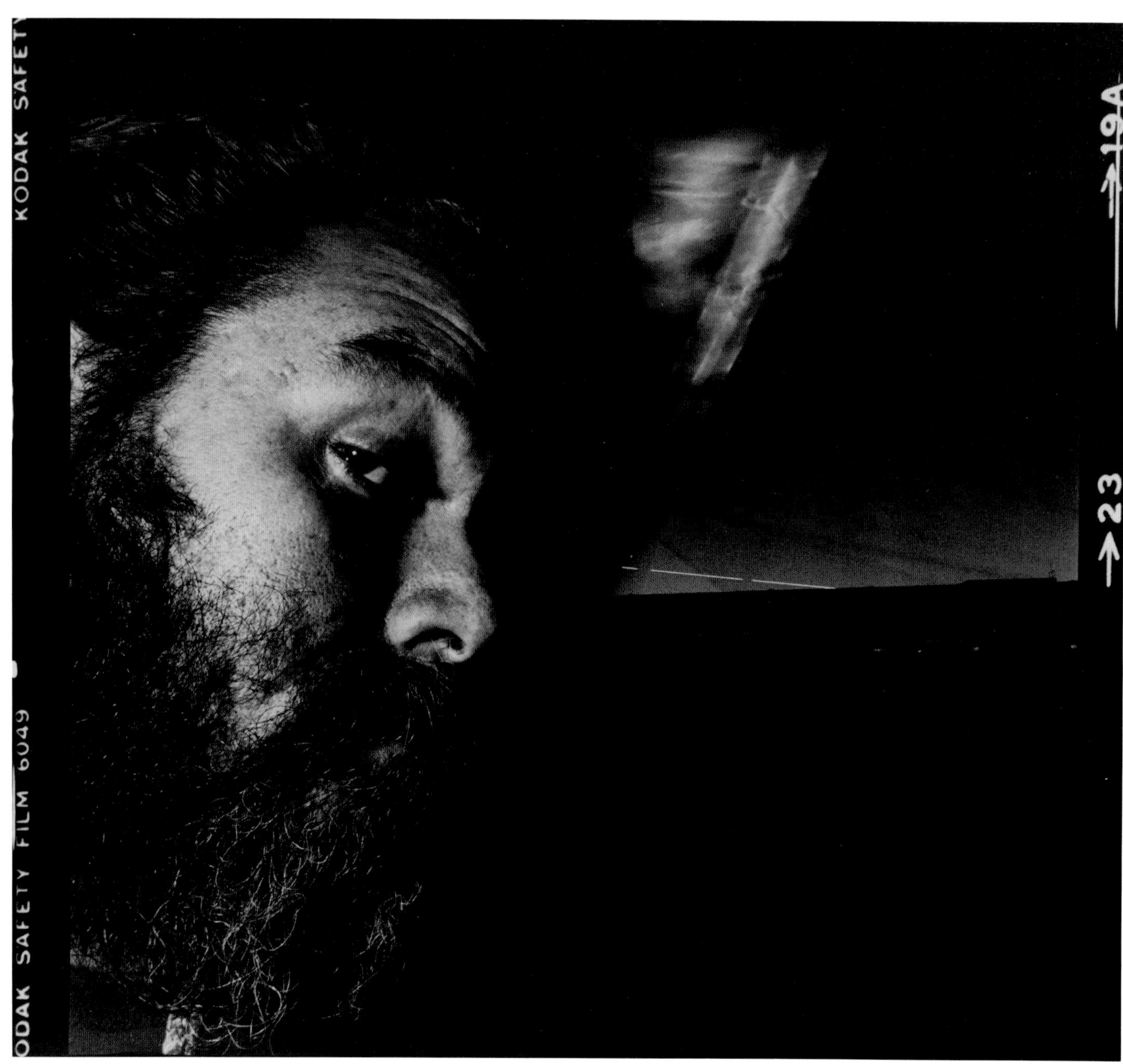

PAUL DIAMOND
133. *Tourist*, 1982

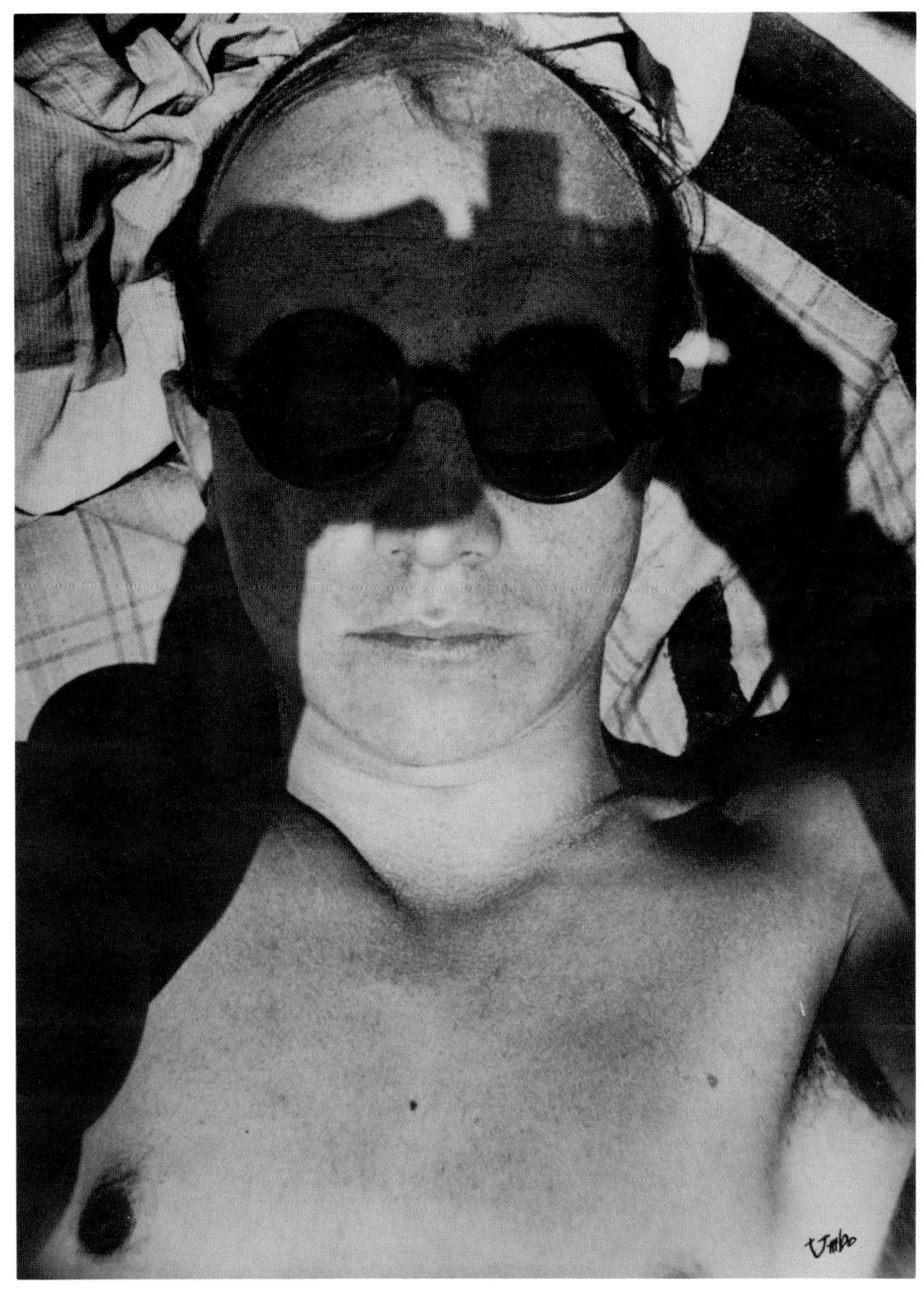

UMBO (Otto Umbehr)
111. *Selbst (Self)*, ca. 1930/1980

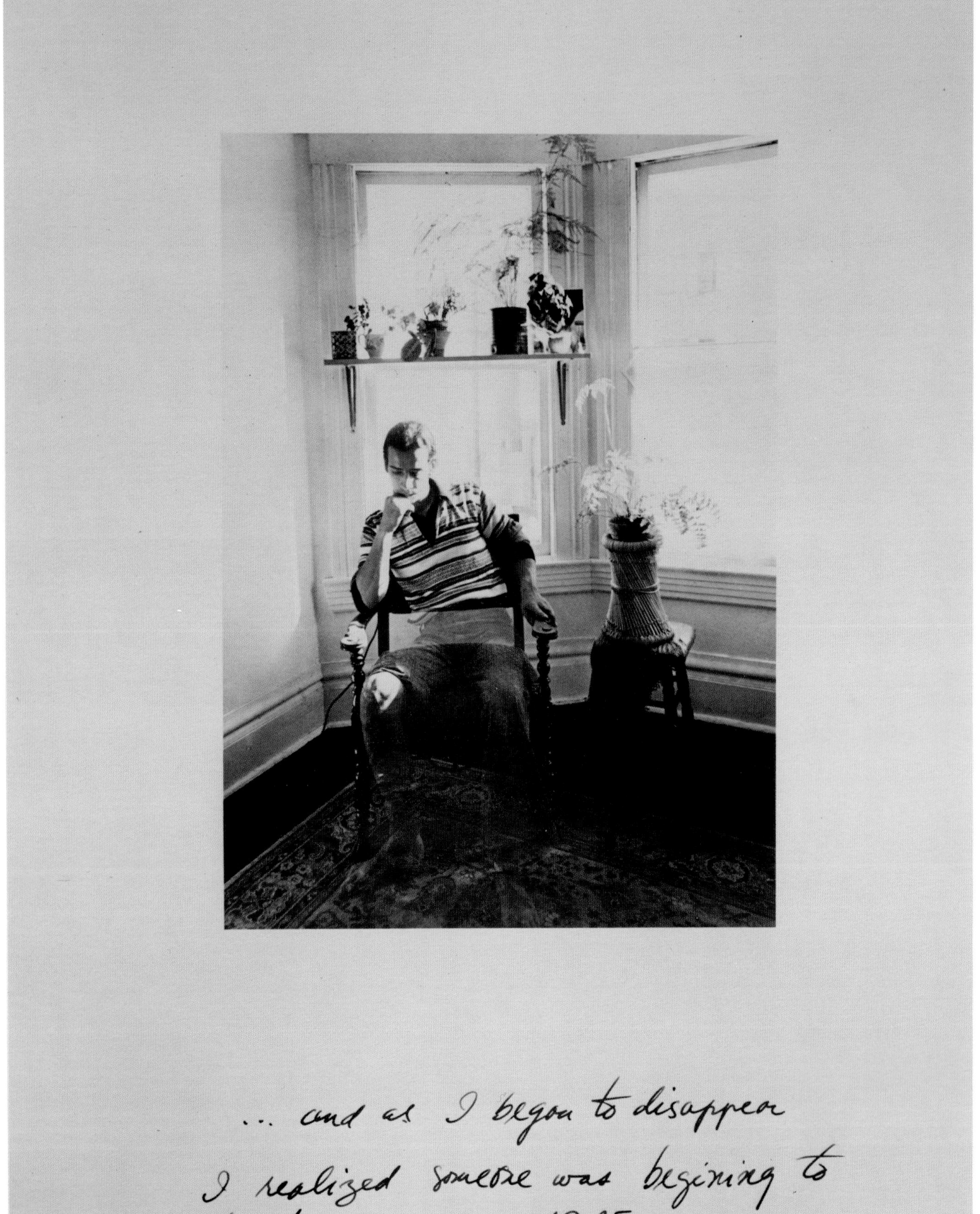

ADÁL (Adál Maldonado)
119. *Visual Exercise I, 1972 / 1973*

Notes

1. Erwin Panofsky, *Studies in Iconology—Humanistic Themes in the Art of the Renaissance*, Harper Torchbooks edition (New York: Harper & Row, 1962), 11. Flannery O'Connor, "The Enduring Chill," *The Complete Stories* (New York: Farrar, Strauss & Giroux, 1971), 362.

2. Director of Photography Van Deren Coke took charge of the collection in 1979 from Curator John Humphrey who had overseen the photography collection since 1935.

3. Susan Sontag, *On Photography* (New York: Farrar, Strauss & Giroux, 1977), 197.

4. Sarah Greenough and Juan Hamilton, *Alfred Stieglitz, Photographs and Writings* (Washington, D.C.: National Gallery of Art; New York: Callaway Editions, 1983), 17.

5. Henri Focillon, *The Life of Forms in Art*, trans. Charles Beecher Hogan and George Kubler, 2nd English ed. enlarged (New York: Wittenborn & Schultz, Inc., 1948), 65. This essay was originally published in French in 1936 under the title "Eloge de la main," for the 2nd French ed. of *Vie des Formes*. It is interesting to note that the historian Walter Benjamin wrote his influential essay "Art in the Age of Mechanical Reproduction" in the same year. It can be seen as a companion piece to the Focillon essay in that it represents the other end of the philosophical spectrum concerning the role of the "machine-made" in the realm of art.

6. Arturo Schwartz, *Man Ray—The Rigour of Imagination* (London: Thames & Hudson, 1977), 136.

7. Van Deren Coke, *Avant-Garde Photography in Germany 1919-1939* (San Francisco: San Francisco Museum of Modern Art, 1980), 30-31.

8. William S. Rubin, *Dada and Surrealist Art* (New York: Harry N. Abrams, Inc., 1968), 342, 469. Rubin writes that New York galleries became the meeting ground for Surrealists in exile especially the Julian Levy Gallery and the Pierre Matisse Gallery. Peggy Guggenheim's gallery, Art of This Century, was also a focal point.

9. Julian Levy was a strong supporter of photography and exhibited it regularly. See: Julian Levy, *Memoir of an Art Gallery* (New York: G. P. Putnam's Sons, 1977), 296-312.

10. Carl Chiarenza, *Aaron Siskind, Pleasures and Terrors* (Boston: Little, Brown & Company, 1982), 57-58.

11. Letter from Jo Ann Callis to author, September 1983.

Checklist of the Exhibition

In the listings of dimensions, height precedes width. Measurements indicate image size; centimeter measurements are given in parentheses. Date refers to the date of the negative; when two are listed and separated by a slash, the second is the date of the print. When known, print edition numbers follow the medium; portfolio edition numbers follow the portfolio title. Where the artist has written the title on the work, it is rendered exactly as inscribed. Alternative titles by which the work may be known as well as those by which it has previously been recorded are given in parentheses and are italicized. If "Untitled" appears in italics, this is the title assigned by the artist; if it does not appear in italics, the work has no title. Descriptive phrases follow untitled works in parentheses. Foreign titles are given in their original language with English translations following in parentheses, also in italics; in the case of highly specialized terminology or where an accurate translation cannot be ascertained, the English translation is not included. All works are gelatin silver prints unless otherwise indicated. All work is from the permanent collection of photography of the San Francisco Museum of Modern Art. Accession numbers appear after the credit line.

The Modern Object

THEO BALLMER
Swiss   1902–1965

1. Untitled (machine, pulleys, hooks), ca. 1932, gelatin silver print (negative image), 8¼ x 11¹¹⁄₁₆" (20.9 x 29.7), Purchase, 82.332

ILSE BING
American   born Germany 1899

2. *Telegraph Pole, Frankfurt, Germany,* 1929, 7⅞ x 5⅝" (20.0 x 14.3), Gift of Simon and Patricia Lowinsky, 82.301

3. *Fokker Airplane,* 1933, 8¹³⁄₁₆ x 11⅛" (22.4 x 28.2), Gift of Robert Shapazian, 81.290

ANTON BRUEHL
American   born Australia
1900–1981

4. *6,000 Watts,* 1927/1978, 13¹⁵⁄₁₆ x 11" (35.4 x 27.9), Byron Meyer Fund Purchase, 79.106

5. *Liner Smoke Stacks (Queen Mary),* 1929, 13¹¹⁄₁₆ x 10¹³⁄₁₆" (34.8 x 27.5), Fund of the 80's Purchase, 84.133

ED CISMONDI
American   born 1917

6. *Engine Form,* 1936/1984, 20/25, 7¼ x 9½" (18.4 x 24.1), Gift of the artist, 84.41

ALFRED EHRHARDT
German   born 1901

7. *Die Deutschland,* 1930, 6⅞ x 9⅜" (17.5 x 23.8), Foto Forum Purchase, Gift of Anne Walker, 84.1735

HANS FINSLER
Swiss   born Germany
1891–1975

8. Untitled (candy), 1920s, 5¹⁄₁₆ x 3¹³⁄₁₆" (12.9 x 9.7), Gift of Paul M. Hertzmann Incorporated, 83.313

9. Untitled ("Sarizol" toothpaste and brush), ca. 1930, 8½ x 6" (21.6 x 15.2), Purchase, 81.141

JAROMÍR FUNKE
Czechoslovakian   1896–1945

10. *Komposition,* bet. 1927–29/1970s, 14⁹⁄₁₆ x 11" (37.0 x 27.9), Mrs. Ferdinand C. Smith Fund Purchase, 80.8

11. *Zbrěnského okruhu (From the Brno Racing Track),* 1930/1970s, 10¹³⁄₁₆ x 9¾" (27.5 x 24.8), Mrs. Ferdinand C. Smith Fund Purchase, 80.6

12. *Fabrik (Factory),* 1932/1970s, from the series, *Mein Koln (My Cologne),* 11 x 10⅞" (27.9 x 27.6), Mrs. Ferdinand C. Smith Fund Purchase, 80.7

HEIN GORNY
German   1904–1967

13. Untitled (collars), 1928/1980, 10⅝ x 7⅞" (27.0 x 20.0), Gift of Joachim Giesel, 82.355

14. Untitled (cars), ca. 1930/1980, 10⅝ x 7⅞" (27.0 x 20.0), Gift of Joachim Giesel, 82.354

JOHN HAVINDEN
English   born 1908

15. Untitled (magnetic fields), ca. 1930, 9⁵⁄₁₆ x 7⅜" (23.7 x 18.8), Fund of the 80's Purchase, 84.145

16. *Linesman, General Post Office,* ca. 1932–34, 9⅜ x 7⅜" (23.8 x 18.8), Purchase, 83.28

FRANÇOIS KOLLAR
French   born Hungary
1904–1979

17. Untitled (tennis racket factory), 1932, 10¼ x 6³⁄₁₆" (26.0 x 15.7), Gift of Mrs. Virginia M. Zabriskie, 83.340

WERNER MANTZ
German   born 1901

18. *Kölnische Zeitung Pressa (Cologne Newspaper Press),* 1928, from the portfolio, *Werner Mantz: 10 Photografien 1927–1935 (Werner Mantz: 10 Photographs 1927–1935),* 1977, 16/25, 7⁹⁄₁₆ x 8⅞" (19.2 x 21.4), Mrs. Ferdinand C. Smith Fund Purchase, 80.1.9

PAUL OUTERBRIDGE
American   1896–1958

19. *Crankshaft Silhouetted Against Car,* 1923, platinum print, 1⁷⁄₁₆ x 4¹⁄₁₆" (4.7 x 10.3), Purchase, 82.336

ROGER PARRY
French   1905–1977

20. Untitled (train signal), ca. 1929, from the deluxe edition of *Banalité* by Leon-Paul Fargue, 1930, gelatin silver print with toner, 8⅝ x 6⁹⁄₁₆" (21.9 x 16.7), Gift of Robert Shapazian, 82.540

21. Untitled (train), ca. 1930, from the book, *Banalité,* 77/300, 1930, collotype, (negative image), 8⅝ x 6⅝" (21.9 x 16.8), Gift of Robert Shapazian, 82.488.2

ALBERT RENGER-PATZSCH
German   1897–1966

22. *Winderhitzer im Hochofen Herrenwyk,* 1927/1979, 9¹⁄₁₆ x 6¹¹⁄₁₆" (23.0 x 17.0), The Helen Crocker Russell and William H. and Ethel W. Crocker Family Funds Purchase, 80.13

ADOLF SCHNEEBERGER
Czechoslovakian   1897–1977

23. *Eivky,* 1931, 9⅜ x 9⅛" (23.8 x 23.2), Foto Forum Purchase, Gift of Anne Walker, 84.1736

ANTON STANKOWSKI
German   born 1906

24. *1/100 sec bei 70 km/h (1/100 sec at 70 km/hr),* 1930/1980, 8⁷⁄₁₆ x 6¹⁵⁄₁₆" (21.4 x 17.6), Purchase, 81.144

25. *Nagel (Nails),* 1930, gelatin silver print (negative image), 3³⁄₁₆ x 4⁵⁄₁₆" (8.1 x 11.0), Purchase, 82.341

26. *Nagel (Nails),* 1930/later print, 7 x 9⁷⁄₁₆" (17.8 x 24.0), Gift of the artist, 82.364

27. *Zurcher Brechkoks (Zurich Crushed Coal),* 1931, two-color, half-tone photomontage leaflet with text, unfolded: 13 x 18⅞" (33.0 x 47.9), Purchase, 82.339

EDWARD STEICHEN
American   born Luxembourg
1879–1973

28. *The George Washington Bridge, New York,* 1931, 9¹¹⁄₁₆ x 7⅝" (24.6 x 19.4), Gift of Mr. and Mrs. Martin Bovill, 84.1436

RALPH STEINER
American   born 1899

29. *Typewriter,* 1921-22/1982, 8⅛ x 6¹⁄₁₆" (20.7 x 15.4), Gift of Willard Van Dyke, 83.428

30. Untitled (egg beater, pan and elongated shadow), from the unique book, *The Beater and the Pan,* 1921–22, each: 4¹¹⁄₁₆ x 3³⁄₁₆" (11.9 x 8.1 cm), Purchase, 83.109.1-8

ALFRED STIEGLITZ
American   1864–1946

31. *The Aeroplane,* 1910/1911, from the quarterly, *Camera Work,* October 1911, photogravure, 5¹¹⁄₁₆ x 6¹⁵⁄₁₆" (14.5 x 17.6), Gift of Graham Nash, 78.229

PAUL STRAND
American   1890–1976

32. *Double Akeley, New York,* 1922, 9¹¹⁄₁₆ x 7¾" (24.6 x 19.7), The Helen Crocker Russell and William H. and Ethel W. Crocker Family Funds Purchase, 80.83

33. *Akeley Motion Picture Camera, New York City,* 1923, from *On My Doorstep: A Portfolio of Eleven Photographs 1915–1973,* 1976, 19/50, 9½ x 7¹¹⁄₁₆" (24.1 x 19.5), Purchase, 77.77

WILLARD VAN DYKE
American   born 1906

34. *Funnels,* ca. 1932/later print, 7 x 9½" (17.8 x 24.1), Purchase, 82.64

BRETT WESTON
American   born 1911

35. Untitled *(Pipes No. 5),* 1927, 9⁵⁄₁₆ x 7" (23.6 x 17.8), Albert M. Bender Collection, Bequest of Albert M. Bender, 41.3000

36. Untitled *(Ford Tri-Motor Plane),* 1935, 7⅝ x 9⁹⁄₁₆" (19.4 x 24.3), The Henry Swift Collection, Gift of Florence Alston Swift, 63.19.141

EDWARD WESTON
American   1886–1958

37. *Pipes and Stacks (Armco Steel, Ohio),* 1922, 9⁷⁄₁₆ x 7⁹⁄₁₆" (24.0 x 19.2), Albert M. Bender Collection, Albert M. Bender Bequest Fund Purchase, 62.1182

38. *Egg Slicer,* ca. 1930, 7⅝ x 9⅛" (19.4 x 23.2), Albert M. Bender Collection, Albert M. Bender Bequest Fund Purchase, 62.1159

The Disembodied Human Figure

MEHEMED FEHMY AGHA
American   born Russia
1896–1978

39. Untitled (bust with wooden model), ca. 1930, 4⁷⁄₁₆ x 3¹¹⁄₁₆″ (11.3 x 9.4), Gift of the Modern Art Council in memory of John Dickinson, 82.70

MANUEL ALVAREZ BRAVO
Mexican   born 1902

40. *Dos Pares de Piernas (Two Pairs of Legs)*, 1928–29, from the portfolio, *Photographs by Manuel Alvarez Bravo*, 1977, 28/100, 9¼ x 7³⁄₈″ (23.5 x 18.3), Gift of Dr. and Mrs. Lawrence Goldmuntz, 80.227.10

THEO BALLMER
Swiss   1902–1965

41. Untitled (hands and drafting tools), ca. 1932, 7³⁄₈ x 5¹⁄₈″ (18.3 x 13.0), Purchase, 82.333

42. Untitled (hands, ruler, clip), ca. 1932, 11⁹⁄₁₆ x 8¹¹⁄₁₆″ (29.4 x 22.1), Purchase, 82.331

HANS BELLMER
German   1902–1975

43. Untitled (legs, lace, rose, and shoe), from the book, *La Poupée (The Doll)*, 1936, 6³⁄₄ x 5¹⁄₈″ (17.1 x 13.0), Purchase, 82.57.10

44. *La Mitrailleuse en État de Grâce (The Machine Gun in a State of Grace)*, 1937, gelatin silver print with paint, 25½ x 25½″ (64.7 x 64.7), Foto Forum Purchase, 84.123

RUTH BERNHARD
American   born Germany 1905

45. *Doll's Head (Creation)*, 1936, 7³⁄₈ x 9¼″ (18.7 x 23.5), The Helen Crocker Russell and William H. and Ethel W. Crocker Family Funds Purchase, 80.178

AENNE BIERMANN
German   1898–1933

46. *Schlafende (Sleeping Woman)*, ca. 1929, 6¹⁵⁄₁₆ x 9¹⁄₈″ (17.6 x 23.2), The Helen Crocker Russell and William H. and Ethel W. Crocker Family Funds Purchase, 80.342

47. *Villa Trauenhand*, 1931, 4¹¹⁄₁₆ x 6⁵⁄₈″ (11.9 x 16.8), Purchase, 82.12

ERWIN BLUMENFELD
American   born Germany 1897–1969

48. *Manina*, 1936/ca. 1947, gelatin silver print (solarized), 13 x 10¼″ (33.0 x 26.0), Mrs. Ferdinand C. Smith Fund Purchase, 78.169

49. Untitled (throat, Paris), 1937, 13½ x 10¾″ (34.3 x 27.3), Foto Forum Purchase, Gift of Anne Walker, 84.1748

50. *Cecil Beaton*, ca. 1937, gelatin silver print (solarized), 12³⁄₈ x 9⁷⁄₈″ (32.4 x 24.0), Purchase, 83.26

51. Untitled (woman's face), ca. 1940, gelatin silver print (solarized), 13¹⁄₈ x 10³⁄₁₆″ (33.3 x 25.9), Mrs. Ferdinand C. Smith Fund Purchase, 79.92

PIERRE BOUCHER
French   born 1908

52. *Ondine*, 1938, gelatin silver print photomontage, 11½ x 9″ (29.2 x 22.9), Gift of Mrs. Virginia M. Zabriskie, 83.262

MARIANNE BRESLAUER
German   born 1909

53. Untitled (Paul Citroen, Berlin), ca. 1927, 7⁷⁄₈ x 5¹¹⁄₁₆″ (20.0 x 14.4), Purchase, 81.41

ANTON BRUEHL
American   born Australia 1900–1981

54. Untitled (male model), 1929/bet. 1979–84, 13¹¹⁄₁₆ x 10¹³⁄₁₆″ (34.8 x 27.5), Fund of the 80's Purchase, 84.134

FRANCIS BRUGUIÈRE
American   1879–1945

55. Untitled (Sebastian Droste), bet. 1923–25, from the *Francis Bruguière Portfolio*, 1977, 1/15, 9½ x 7¼″ (24.1 x 18.4), Mrs. Ferdinand C. Smith Fund Purchase, 78.26

56. Untitled (Rosalinde Fuller and Lance Sievking), ca. 1929, from the *Francis Bruguière Portfolio*, 1977, 1/15, 9⁷⁄₈ x 7³⁄₈″ (24.0 x 18.7), Mrs. Ferdinand C. Smith Fund Purchase, 78.23

57. Oswell Blakeston, ca. 1934–35, 11 x 13½″ (27.9 x 34.3), Fund of the 80's Purchase, 84.135

HORACIO COPPOLA
Argentinian   born 1907

58. *Grossmutter Puppe (Grandmother's Doll)*, 1932, 6½ x 6¹³⁄₁₆″ (16.5 x 17.3 cm), Purchase, 81.42

IMOGEN CUNNINGHAM
American   born 1883–1976

59. *Martha Graham*, 1931, 5³⁄₄ x 7⁵⁄₈″ (14.6 x 19.4), The Henry Swift Collection, Gift of Florence Alston Swift, 63.19.182

WALKER EVANS
American   1903–1975

60. Untitled (variation of *Votive Candles, New York City*), ca. 1929, 9½ x 6¼″ (24.1 x 15.9), Margery Mann Memorial Collection, Gift of Tom Vasey, 80.161

ANDREAS FEININGER
American   born France 1906

62. *Herbert List*, 1930/1981, 9³⁄₈ x 7¹⁄₁₆″ (23.8 x 17.9), Purchase, 82.6

LOUIS FAURER
American   born 1916

61. *Philadelphia, Pa.*, 1937, 13³⁄₈ x 8⁷⁄₈″ (34.0 x 22.6), Fund of the 80's Purchase, 84.139

WERNER DAVID FEIST
Canadian   born Germany 1909

63. *Man with Pipe*, 1928, 7⁷⁄₈ x 5⁵⁄₈″ (20.0 x 14.3), Purchase, 82.7

64. Untitled (M. (?) Bahelfer), 1929, 3⁷⁄₈ x 3″ (9.8 x 7.6), Purchase, 81.46

HANS FINSLER
Swiss   born Germany 1891–1975

65. Untitled (mirror reflecting legs), bet. 1922-33, 6⁵⁄₈ x 4⁹⁄₁₆″ (16.8 x 11.6), Purchase, 82.22

GEORGE HURRELL
American   born 1904

66. *Douglas Fairbanks*, ca. 1930-33/ca. 1980, from the portfolio, *Hurrell II*, 1980, 97/250, 19 x 15¹¹⁄₁₆″ (48.2 x 39.8 cm), Gift of Stanford Blume, 81.321.5

67. *Joan Crawford*, ca. 1930–33, from the portfolio, *Hurrell*, 1980, 49/250, 18⁷⁄₈ x 15⁵⁄₈″ (47.9 x 39.7), Gift of Stanley M. Miller, 81.322.3

LOTTE JACOBI
American   born Germany 1896

68. *Franz Lederer*, ca. 1929/bet. 1978–79, 8¹³⁄₁₆ x 6″ (22.4 x 15.2), Gift of the artist, 82.306

69. *Head of a Dancer, Berlin*, 1929/bet. 1978–79, 7¹¹⁄₁₆ x 9⁵⁄₈″ (19.5 x 24.4), Gift of the artist, 82.308

70. *Lotte Lenya*, ca. 1930/bet. 1978–79, 7⁹⁄₁₆ x 8¹⁵⁄₁₆″ (19.2 x 22.7), Gift of the artist, 82.307

ANDRÉ KERTÉSZ
American   born Hungary 1894

71. Untitled (fortune teller), 1927, 6¹⁄₈ x 7⁵⁄₈″ (15.6 x 19.4 cm), Purchase, 79.261

72. *Distortion No. 4 (Paris)*, 1933/ca. 1975, 9³⁄₄ x 7⁷⁄₁₆″ (24.8 x 18.9 cm), Gift of Graham Nash, 79.389

73. *Distortion No. 102 (Paris)*, 1933/ca. 1975, 9¹³⁄₁₆ x 7³⁄₁₆″ (24.9 x 18.3 cm), Gift of Graham Nash, 79.391

EDMUND KESTING
German   1892–1970

74. Untitled *(Face Solarization)*, 1928, gelatin silver print (solarized), 8³⁄₈ x 7″ (21.3 x 17.8), The Helen Crocker Russell and William H. and Ethel W. Crocker Family Purchase, 80.183

FRANÇOIS KOLLAR
French   born Hungary 1904–1979

75. *Bord de Mer (Seashore)*, 1930, 19½ x 15⁵⁄₈″ (49.5 x 39.7), Purchase, 79.249

76. *Le Tabac (Tobacco)*, 1934, gelatin silver print (photogram), 11 x 8¹¹⁄₁₆″ (27.9 x 22.1), The Helen Crocker Russell and William H. and Ethel W. Crocker Family Funds Purchase, 80.19

77. Untitled (woman wearing pearls), 1934 (for *Harper's Bazaar*), 11 x 8½″ (27.9 x 21.6), Mortimer Fleishhacker, Jr., Memorial Fund Purchase, 80.400

YASUO KUNIYOSHI
American   born Japan 1893–1953

78. *Coney Island*, 1938, 9¹⁄₁₆ x 7¹⁄₁₆″ (23.0 x 17.9), Gift of Mrs. Yasuo Kuniyoshi, 84.421

DOROTHEA LANGE
American   1895–1965

79. Untitled (circular hair braids), 1930s, 3⁷⁄₈ x 3³⁄₄″ (9.8 x 9.5), Gift of Tom Vasey, 82.45

NATHAN LERNER
American   born 1913

80. *Screen and Hand*, 1940, 10¹³⁄₁₆ x 14″ (27.5 x 35.5 cm), Gift of Graham Nash, 79.398

HELMAR LERSKI
German   1871–1956

81. Untitled (close-up of a man's face), 1936, from the series, *Metamorphosis through Light*, 11½ x 9″ (29.2 x 22.8), Foto Forum Purchase, 85.6

ALICE LEX-NERLINGER
German   born 1893

82. *Arbeiten, Arbeiten, Arbeiten (Work, Work, Work)*, 1928, 8 x 6³⁄₄″ (20.3 x 17.1), Gift of Robert Shapazian, 81.331

W.M. HEINZ LOEW
British   born Germany 1903–1982

83. Untitled (man with superimposed shadow), 1927/1980, 10⁵⁄₈ x 7⁷⁄₈″ (27.0 x 20.0), Purchase, 81.35

GEORGE PLATT LYNES
American   1907–1955

84. *Yves Tanguy*, ca. 1938, 9³⁄₁₆ x 7⁷⁄₁₆″ (23.3 x 19.2), Fund of the 80's Purchase, 84.268

MAN RAY
American   1890–1976

85. Untitled (hand and key), 1922, gelatin silver print (Rayograph), 11¹⁵⁄₁₆ x 9³⁄₈″ (30.3 x 23.8), Purchase, 82.151

86. *André Breton*, ca. 1930, 9¹⁄₈ x 7¹⁄₈″ (23.2 x 18.1), Purchase, 84.57

87. Untitled (cast self-portrait with mannequin hands, lightbulb, and polyhedron), 1933, 11⁹⁄₁₆ x 9¹⁄₁₆″ (29.4 x 23.0), The Helen Crocker Russell and William H. and Ethel W. Crocker Family Funds Purchase, 80.344

88. Untitled (Elsa Schiaparelli), 1933, 9⁷⁄₁₆ x 7³⁄₁₆″ (24.0 x 18.3), The Helen Crocker Russell and William H. and Ethel W. Crocker Family Funds Purchase, 80.348

LUCIA MOHOLY
British   born in Czech-speaking Austria, ca. 1900

89. *Franz Roh, Art Historian*, ca. 1926/1980, 15⁷⁄₈ x 12″ (40.3 x 30.5), Gift of the artist, 82.311

ROGER PARRY
French   1905–1977

90. Untitled (bottles and glove), ca. 1929, from the deluxe edition of *Banalité* by Leon-Paul Fargue, 1930, gelatin silver print with toner, 8⁵⁄₈ x 6⁹⁄₁₆″ (21.9 x 16.7), Gift of Robert Shapazian, 82.539

91. Untitled (man and gun), ca. 1929, from the deluxe edition of *Banalité* by Leon-Paul Fargue, 1930, gelatin silver print with toner, 8¹⁄₁₆ x 6⁹⁄₁₆″ (20.5 x 16.7), Gift of Robert Shapazian, 82.538

92. Untitled (two superimposed faces), ca. 1930, 8⁷⁄₈ x 6⁵⁄₈″ (22.5 x 16.8), Purchase, 83.32

WALTER PETERHANS
German   born 1897–1960

93. Untitled (still life with gloves),
1926–36, from *Walter Peterhans:
A Portfolio of Ten Photographs*,
1977, 2/35, 10³/₄ x 12⁷/₁₆"
(27.3 x 31.6), Mrs. Ferdinand
C. Smith Fund Purchase, 79.208

WERNER ROHDE
German   born 1906

94. *Self-Portrait*, 1929, 6⁵/₈ x 4¹¹/₁₆"
(16.8 x 11.9), Fund of the 80's
Purchase, 84.157

HAJO ROSE (Hans-Joachim)
German   born 1910

95. Untitled (jumping man superimposed over face), ca. 1928,
6³/₈ x 4¹/₄" (16.2 x 10.8),
Purchase, 82.63

ADOLF SCHNEEBERGER
Czechoslovakian   1897–1977

96. *Komposični Studie (Composition
Study)*, 1927, 11³/₈ x 8⁷/₈"
(28.9 x 22.5), Mrs. Ferdinand
C. Smith Fund Purchase, 80.2

HERBERT SCHÜRMANN
German   1908–1982

97. Untitled (hands and hair against
fabric), bet. 1931–33, 6⁷/₁₆ x 8⁷/₈"
(16.3 x 22.5), Purchase, 83.160

ANTON STANKOWSKI
German   born 1906

98. *Schattenstufen (Shadow Steps)*,
1932, 8¹¹/₁₆ x 6⁷/₈" (22.1 x 17.5),
Purchase, 84.31

EDWARD STEICHEN
American   born Luxembourg
1879–1973

99. *Goethe Mask (Mask of Goethe
and Spiral)*, 1932, 13⁷/₈ x 10¹³/₁₆"
(35.2 x 27.5), Bequest of
Edward Steichen, 82.146

ALFRED STIEGLITZ
American   1864–1946

100. *Georgia O'Keeffe*, 1920, palladium
print, 9³/₈ x 7⁹/₁₆" (23.8 x 19.2),
Alfred Stieglitz Collection,
Purchase, 52.1813

101. *Georgia O'Keeffe*, 1922, palladium
print, 7³/₄ x 9¹/₂" (19.7 x 24.1),
Alfred Stieglitz Collection,
Gift of Georgia O'Keeffe, 52.1814

102. Untitled (Katherine Dudley, feet),
1922, palladium print,
7¹/₂ x 9⁵/₁₆" (19.0 x 23.6),
Alfred Stieglitz Collection,
Purchase, 52.1799

103. *Dorothy Norman*, ca. 1931–32,
4³/₈ x 3⁵/₈" (11.1 x 9.2),
Alfred Stieglitz Collection,
Gift of Georgia O'Keeffe, 52.1849

HENRY SWIFT
American   1890–1960

104. Untitled (hand and toy), 1930s,
4¹¹/₁₆ x 3³/₈" (11.9 x 8.6), The
Henry Swift Collection, Gift of
Florence Alston Swift, 63.19.162

MAURICE TABARD
French   1897–1984

105. *Portrait of the Dancer George
Pomies*, 1929, 8⁷/₈ x 6⁹/₁₆"
(22.5 x 16.7), Gift of Robert
Shapazian, 82.556

106. Untitled (overlapping negative
and positive images of a woman's
face), 1929, 6¹¹/₁₆ x 4⁷/₁₆"
(17.0 x 11.3), Purchase, 81.34

TATO (Guglielmo Sansoni)
Italian   1896–1974

107. *Ritratto Meccanico di Remo Chiti
(Mechanical Portrait of Remo
Chiti)*, 1930, 9³/₈ x 7"
(23.8 x 17.8), Byron Meyer
Fund Purchase, 83.19

UMBO (Otto Umbehr)
German   1902–1980

108. *Rut Maske (Die Larve) (Rut Maske
[The Mask])*, 1927, from the
Umbo Portfolio, 1980, 34/50,
7¹/₁₆ x 5¹/₁₆" (17.9 x 12.9),
Purchase, 83.36.3

109. *Traümende (The Dreamers)*,
1928–29, from the *Umbo Portfolio*, 1980, 34/50, 8⁵/₁₆ x 11⁹/₁₆"
(21.1 x 29.4), Purchase,
83.36.7

110. *Pantoffeln (Slippers)*, ca. 1928–
29, from the *Umbo Portfolio*,
1980, 34/50, 9⁷/₁₆ x 6⁷/₈"
(24.0 x 17.5), Purchase, 83.36.1

111. *Selbst (Self)*, ca. 1930, from the
Umbo Portfolio, 1980, 34/50,
11¹/₂ x 8¹¹/₁₆" (29.2 x 22.1),
Purchase, 83.36.5

EDWARD WESTON
American   1886–1958

112. *Knees*, 1927, 6¹/₄ x 9³/₁₆"
(15.9 x 23.3), Albert M.
Bender Collection, Bequest
of Albert M. Bender, 41.2993

YVA (Else Simon)
German   1900–1942

113. *Hands Study*, ca. 1928, 7³/₄ x 5⁵/₈"
(19.7 x 14.3 cm), Purchase, 81.23

114. Untitled (legs and shoes), 1929,
8⁷/₈ x 6³/₈" (22.5 x 16.2 cm),
Purchase, 81.24

ADÁL (Adál Maldonado)
American   born Puerto Rico 1947

115. *Peso de Orgullo (Weight of
Pride)*, ca. 1972, from the untitled
portfolio by L.R. John and Adál,
1973, 1/6, 5¹¹/₁₆ x 7¹³/₁₆"
(14.4 x 19.8), Anonymous gift,
73.42.13

116. *Continuing Saga of 665 West End
Ave.*, 1972, from the untitled portfolio by L.R. John and Adál, 1973,
1/6, 6¹³/₁₆ x 4¹³/₁₆" (17.3 x 12.2),
Anonymous gift, 73.42.16

117. *Logic of Limitations*, 1972, from
the untitled portfolio by L.R. John
and Adál, 1973, 1/6, 6¹³/₁₆ x 6³/₈"
(17.3 x 16.2), Anonymous gift,
73.42.17

118. *Evidence of Things not Seen*, ca.
1972, from the untitled portfolio
by L.R. John and Adál, 1973,
1/6, 6⁷/₈ x 6³/₈" (17.5 x 16.2),
Anonymous gift, 73.42.18

119. *Visual Exercise I*, 1972, from
the untitled portfolio by L.R.
John and Adál, 1973, 1/6,
7³/₄ x 5⁵/₈" (19.7 x 14.3 cm),
Anonymous Gift, 73.42.20

120. *Trajic Joke*, 1973, from the untitled
portfolio by L.R. John and Adál,
1973, 1/6, 6¹⁵/₁₆ x 6³/₄" (17.6 x 17.1),
Anonymous gift, 73.42.19

LUCIEN AIGNER
American   born Hungary 1901

121. Untitled (woman in dressing
room), ca. 1940/1970,
12¹¹/₁₆ x 10¹/₁₆" (32.2 x 25.6),
Anonymous gift, 80.463

ELEANOR ANTIN
American   born 1935

122. *100 Boots in the Park*, 1973, from
the series, *100 Boots*, 1971-73,
51 half-tone photo-postcards
(photographs by Philip Steinmetz),
4¹/₂ x 7" (11.4 x 17.8),
Anonymous gift, 83.116.1-51

RUTH BERNHARD
American   born Germany 1905

123. *One World*, 1946/ca. 1982,
10⁵/₁₆ x 13¹/₂" (26.2 x 34.3),
Gift of the artist, 83.117

DIANA BLOK
MARLO BROEKMANS
Uruguayan   born 1952
Dutch   born 1953

124. *Mirror*, 1980, 11¹/₁₆ x 8⁵/₁₆"
(28.1 x 21.1), Purchase, 84.20

BILL BRANDT
British   1904–1983

125. *Portrait of a Young Girl
(Eaton Place, London)*, 1955,
13⁷/₁₆ x 11¹¹/₁₆" (34.1 x 29.7),
Purchase, 74.43

WYNN BULLOCK
American   1902–1975

126. *The Dress*, 1956, 9⁹/₁₆ x 7⁷/₁₆"
(24.3 x 18.9), Anonymous gift,
69.58.14

NANCY BURSON
American   born 1948

127. *Mankind* (computer-generated
portrait of three major races pro-
portioned to reflect current popu-
lation statistics), 1983, 7¹⁵/₁₆ x 7¹/₂"
(20.2 x 19.0), Fund of the 80's
Purchase, 84.262

JACK BUTLER
American   born 1947

128. *Excitable Pages Series #6*,
1978, Cibachrome with oil,
15¹⁵/₁₆ x 19¹⁵/₁₆" (40.5 x 50.6),
Gift of G. Austin Conkey, 84.73

JO ANN CALLIS
American   born 1940

129. *Man in Tie*, 1976, from *Silver See:
A Portfolio of Photography from
Los Angeles*, 1977, ed. 45, Ekta-
color print, 9¹/₈ x 7" (23.2 x 17.8),
Mrs. Ferdinand C. Smith
Fund Purchase, 78.171.1

MARK COHEN
American   born 1943

130. Untitled (people on sidewalk),
1974, 11³/₁₆ x 17¹¹/₁₆" (30.0 x
44.9), Helen Crocker Russell
Memorial Fund Purchase, 80.393

131. Untitled (girl with jump rope),
1975/1976, 12¹/₁₆ x 17⁷/₈"
(30.6 x 45.4), Mrs. Ferdinand
C. Smith Fund Purchase, 80.394

KONRAD CRAMER
American   born Germany
1888–1963

132. Untitled (pitcher with paint
brushes and classical head),
ca. 1946, gelatin silver print
(negative image), 9⁵/₈ x 7¹³/₁₆"
(24.4 x 19.8), Purchase, 83.167

PAUL DIAMOND
American   born 1942

133. *Tourist*, 1982, 15⁹/₁₆ x 19¹¹/₁₆"
(39.5 x 50.0), Fund of the 80's
Purchase, 84.136

KEN DOMON
Japanese   born 1909

134. *Bunraku (Puppet #2)*, ca. 1941–
42, 10³/₄ x 8³/₁₆" (27.3 x 20.8),
Anonymous gift, 80.229

ELLIOTT ERWITT
American   born France 1928

135. Untitled (legs on a wall), 1978/ca.
1979, 11¹³/₁₆ x 8" (30.0 x 20.3),
Gift of Mr. and Mrs. Rene
R.E. Woolcott, 83.195

LEE FRIEDLANDER
American   born 1934

136. *T.V. in Hotel Room—Galax, Virginia*,
1962, from the portfolio, *Fifteen
Photographs by Lee Friedlander*,
1973, 59/75, gelatin silver print
with toner, 5¹³/₁₆ x 8⁷/₈"
(14.8 x 22.5), William L.
Gerstle Collection, William L.
Gerstle Fund Purchase, 74.2.1

137. *Self-Portrait* (Wilmington,
Delaware), 1965, 11¹/₄ x 7⁹/₁₆"
(28.6 x 19.2), Purchase, 84.27

138. *Shadow—New York City*, 1966,
from the portfolio, *Fifteen Photographs by Lee Friedlander*, 1973,
59/75, gelatin silver print with
toner, 6¹/₄ x 9⁷/₁₆" (15.9 x 24.0),
William L. Gerstle Collection,
William L. Gerstle Fund Purchase,
74.2.7

139. *New Orleans*, 1972, 7³/₈ x 13⁷/₈"
(18.9 x 35.2), Fund of the
80's Purchase, 84.143

PHILLIP GALGIANI
American   born 1951

140. *3 Legged Table*, 1977/1978,
14³/₈ x 18¹/₁₆" (36.5 x 45.9),
Soap Box Derby Fund Purchase,
80.395

RALPH GIBSON
American   born 1939

141. Untitled (woman's face obscured
by shadow), 1974, 12¾ x 8³⁄₁₆"
(32.4 x 20.8), Purchase, 82.23

JUDITH GOLDEN
American   born 1934

142. Untitled (paper mask with cut-out
held up to woman's face), 1977,
from Silver See: A Portfolio of
Photography from Los Angeles,
1977, ed. 45, gelatin silver print
with chalk and oil pastels selec-
tively bleached, 13⅞ x 10⅞"
(35.2 x 27.6), Mrs. Ferdinand
C. Smith Fund Purchase, 78.171.6

143. Self-Portrait Fantasy Series #6,
"Time" Cover, Diane Keaton,
1978, gelatin silver print with
oil paint, oil pastel, and ribbon,
21¼ x 19¼" (54.0 x 48.9),
Mrs. Ferdinand C. Smith Fund
Purchase, 79.38

PHILLIPE HALSMANN
American   born Latvia
1906–1979

144. Mao-Marilyn, 1950s, 13¹³⁄₁₆ x 10⅞"
(35.1 x 27.6), Gift of Graham
Nash, 79.383

ANTHONY HERNANDEZ
American   born 1947

145. Untitled (Saigon, Vietnam), 1972,
7¹³⁄₁₆ x 11¹³⁄₁₆" (19.8 x 30.0),
Gift of Joan Murray, 83.335

LEO HOLUB
American   born 1916

146. Billboard, South San Francisco,
1972/1978, 8¾ x 13⅛"
(22.2 x 33.3), Gift of Kit
Monroe Pravda in memory
of Christian Pravda, 78.55

J.P. HUTTO
American   born 1952

147. Dogs Dressed as Men, 1981/1983,
15½ x 19¾" (39.4 x 50.1),
Clinton Walker Fund
Purchase, 84.29

JOSEPH D. JACHNA
American   born 1935

148. Door County, Wisc., 1970,
6¾ x 10" (17.1 x 25.4), Gift
of Mr. and Mrs. Andrew Gilbert,
84.95

149. Dowdy Lake, Colorado
(Ginny's Feet), 1974, 7¼ x 11"
(18.4 x 27.9), Gift of Mr. and
Mrs. Andrew Gilbert, 84.96

HAROLD JONES
American   born 1940

150. Self-Portrait with Water,
1978/1980, 17⅞ x 14³⁄₁₆"
(45.4 x 36.0), Purchase, 81.194

WILLIAM KLEIN
American   born 1928

151. Hand, Lebanon, 1963/1980,
11³⁄₈ x 17⅛" (28.9 x 43.5),
Purchase, 82.334

VILEM KRIZ
American   born Czechoslovakia
1921

152. Sirague City, 1947/1970,
gelatin silver print with toner,
13⁹⁄₁₆ x 10³⁄₈" (34.4 x 26.3),
Gift of the artist, 71.19.8

153. Berkeley, 1964, gelatin silver print
with toner, 13½ x 10⅝"
(34.3 x 27.0), Gift of the
artist, 71.19.4

154. Berkeley, 1969, gelatin silver print
with toner, 13⁵⁄₁₆ x 10³⁄₈"
(33.8 x 26.3), Gift of the
artist, 71.19.1

MICHEL SZULC KRZYZANOWSKI
Dutch   born 1949

155. Zagora (10 januari 1978), 1978,
six gelatin silver prints, each:
4¹⁄₁₆ x 6¹⁄₁₆" (10.3 x 15.4),
overall: 32 x 40¹⁄₁₆"
(81.3 x 101.8), Gift of
Mrs. Virginia M. Zabriskie,
83.343

VICTOR LANDWEBER
American   born 1943

156. Snakes, Venice, CA., 4th of July,
1979, Cibachrome print,
8¾ x 13⅛" (22.2 x 33.3),
Gift of Louis Landweber, 81.218

NATHAN LERNER
American   born 1913

157. Seeing Mouth—Kozman, 1940,
9 x 7½" (22.9 x 19.0 cm), Foto
Forum Purchase, Gift of Anne
Walker, 84.1742

ALEKSANDRAS MACIJAUSKAS
Lithuanian   born 1938

158. Photographer Jonas Kavelis,
1977, 14 x 11¾" (35.5 x 29.8),
Gift of the artist, 80.316

159. Technokratas, 1977, 13⅛ x 9¾"
(33.3 x 24.8), Gift of the
artist, 80.318

RITA MANDLEMAN
American   born 1950

160. Untitled (blurred image with head
and shoulders of figure at right),
1972, from the portfolio, Fifteen
Photographs from the San Francisco Art Institute, 1972, 15/100,
5⁵⁄₁₆ x 8¹⁄₁₆" (13.5 x 20.5 cm),
Anonymous gift, 73.10.7

MARGERY MANN
American   1919–1977

161. London, 1975, from the series,
Summer Still Lifes, 6⅝ x 9¹⁵⁄₁₆"
(16.8 x 25.2), Gift of the artist,
77.146

162. London (four mannequins), 1975,
from the series, Summer Still Lifes,
6⅝ x 9¹⁵⁄₁₆" (16.8 x 25.2),
Gift of the artist, 77.147

RALPH EUGENE MEATYARD
American   1925–1972

163. Untitled (dolls with fish), ca. 1959,
7¹⁄₁₆ x 6⅞" (17.9 x 17.5),
Anonymous gift, 78.160

164. Untitled (carved stone face), ca.
1960, 5¾ x 5¾" (14.6 x 14.6),
Anonymous gift, 84.430

165. Untitled (boy with mushroom-like
object), 1961, 7⁵⁄₁₆ x 7¾"
(18.6 x 19.7), Anonymous gift,
83.361

RAY K. METZKER
American   born 1931

166. City Whispers, 1981/1983,
5⁷⁄₁₆ x 7⅛" (13.8 x 18.1),
Fund of the 80's Purchase, 84.151

DUANE MICHALS
American   born 1932

167. Claes Oldenberg, 1970, 5 x 7"
(12.7 x 17.8), Fund of the 80's
Purchase, 84.152

JOHN MULVANY
American   born 1937

168. Untitled (four boys at play),
1970, 4⅜ x 6⁹⁄₁₆" (11.1 x 16.7),
Anonymous gift, 80.321

JOYCE NEIMANAS
American   born 1944

169. He said, "Let's be honest and admit
our feelings.", 1976, from The School
of The Art Institute of Chicago,
Graduate Photography Portfolio,
1976, ed. 75, gelatin silver print with
ink and toner, 10⅝ x 13⁷⁄₁₆"
(27.0 x 34.1), Purchase, 76.161

ARNOLD NEWMAN
American   born 1918

170. Jean Dubuffet, 1956, 8¹³⁄₁₆ x 7⅝"
(22.4 x 19.4), Anonymous gift,
84.46

CHARLES OSGOOD
American   born 1941

171. Untitled (distorted faces), ca. 1975,
from the portfolio, Photographs
from the School of The Art Institute
of Chicago, 1975, ed. 75,
6½ x 9½" (16.5 x 24.1),
Arthur W. Barney Bequest Fund
Purchase, 75.116.28

172. Untitled (hands holding
daguerreotype), 1976,
from The School of The Art Institute
of Chicago, Graduate Photography
Portfolio, 1976, ed. 75, 8⅛ x 10¹⁄₈"
(20.6 x 25.7), Purchase, 76.162

BRUCE PATTERSON
American   born 1950

173. Richard Burks, 1976, 13¹⁵⁄₁₆ x 13⅞"
(35.4 x 35.2), Mrs. Ferdinand C.
Smith Fund Purchase, 78.178

DONALD ROSS
American   born 1912

174. Neil Weston's Diving Gear, 1952,
13⅝ x 10¹¹⁄₁₆" (34.6 x 27.1),
Gift of the artist, 79.83

XANTI (ALEXANDER)
SCHAWINSKY
American   born Switzerland
1904–1979

175. Untitled (portrait of Walter
Gropius), 1943, gelatin silver print
(solarized), 8 x 5⅞"
(20.3 x 14.9), Purchase, 84.112

SANDRA SEMCHUK
Canadian   born 1948

176. Series #10, 1982/1983,
five Cibachrome prints, each
approximately 7⁹⁄₁₆ x 9⁷⁄₁₆"
(19.2 x 24.0), Purchase, 83.34A-E

177. Co-operative Series #3,
Roweena and I, Yuma, Arizona,
1983, eleven Cibachrome prints,
each: 7¹⁵⁄₁₆ x 9¹⁵⁄₁₆" (20.2 x 25.2),
Fund of the 80's Purchase, 84.160.A-K

SONIA LANDY SHERIDAN
American   born 1925

178. Sound Images, 1973, tape
recorder, transmission facsimile,
3M, and Xerox, 11 x 8⁹⁄₁₆"
(27.9 x 21.7), Margery Mann
Memorial Collection,
Gift of the artist, 77.237

179. Sonia in Time, 1975, from the
portfolio, Photographs from the
School of The Art Institute of
Chicago, 1975, ed. 75, VQC I
color-in-color powder, 8½ x 8½"
(21.6 x 21.6), Arthur W. Barney
Bequest Fund Purchase, 75.116.32

AARON SISKIND
American   born 1903

180. Gloucester I, 1944, 13⁷⁄₁₆ x 10³⁄₁₆"
(34.1 x 25.9), Richard Y. Dakin
Family Memorial Fund Purchase,
68.25

181. Feet, 1957, 5³⁄₈ x 4⅝"
(13.6 x 11.7), Gift of Virginia
Hassel Ballinger in memory
of Paul Hassel, 73.56.9

HENRY HOLMES SMITH
American   born 1909

182. Growing Up II, 1952,
from Henry Holmes Smith: Center
for Photographic Studies, Portfolio
Two, 1973, ed. 30 proof copies
(printed by Alex Traube),
12¹⁄₁₆ x 8" (30.6 x 20.3),
Mrs. Ferdinand C. Smith Fund
Purchase, 73.39.6

183. Pair II, 1952, from Henry Holmes
Smith: Center for Photographic
Studies, Portfolio Two, 1973, ed.
30 proof copies (printed by Alex
Traube), 12¹⁄₁₆ x 8" (30.6 x 20.3),
Mrs. Ferdinand C. Smith Fund
Purchase, 79.39.3

FREDERICK SOMMER
American   born Italy 1905

184. Untitled (doll legs attached to an
illustration of a man in car), 1950,
9⁹⁄₁₆ x 7⅝" (24.3 x 19.4),
Clinton Walker Fund Purchase,
83.76

EVE SONNEMAN
American   born 1946

185. Portrait of My Lover, Central Park,
New York, 1971, 4¾ x 13⅝"
(12.1 x 34.6), Fund of the 80's
Purchase, 84.165

LARRY SULTAN
American   born 1946

186. Untitled (head and shoulders of a
nude woman partially submerged
in water), 1972, from the portfolio, Fifteen Photographs from the
San Francisco Art Institute, 1972,
15/100, 4¹¹⁄₁₆ x 4⅞" (11.9 x 12.4),
Anonymous gift, 73.10.2

VAL TELBERG
American   born Russia 1910

187. Summer at Lincoln Park, 1945,
6¾ x 4¹¹⁄₁₆" (17.1 x 11.9),
Gift of the artist, 83.127

188. Return to Summer Group Palmetto
Gnome, Variation #1, ca. 1948,
9½ x 7¹⁵⁄₁₆" (24.1 x 20.2),
Purchase, 81.192

189. My Hand, ca. 1950–53,
13⅜ x 9¹⁵⁄₁₆" (34.0 x 25.2),
Gift of the artist, 83.134

190. Rebellion Call, 1953, from the
series, Rebellion, 9¼ x 10⅞"
(23.5 x 27.6), Gift of the artist,
83.135

191. For Anais, ca. 1957, 9⅝ x 7⅝"
(24.4 x 19.4), Gift of the artist,
83.136

EDMUND TESKE
American   born 1911

192. Untitled (cupid), ca. 1961, gelatin silver print (solarized), 6⁵⁄₈ x 4⁵⁄₈" (16.8 x 11.7), Purchase with the aid of funds from Reese Palley, 68.50.4

193. Untitled (George Hermes and mask), ca 1964, 15/100, 6³⁄₄ x 4⁵⁄₈" (17.1 x 11.7), Purchased with the aid of funds from Reese Palley, 68.50.2

RUTH THORNE-THOMSEN
American   born 1943

194. *Face at Tulum*, 1979, gelatin silver print with toner, 3³⁄₈ x 4³⁄₈" (8.6 x 11.1 cm), Gift of the artist, 79.154

195. Untitled (sculpted head in profile), 1979, gelatin silver print with toner, 3⁵⁄₈ x 4⁵⁄₁₆" (9.2 x 11.0), Gift of the artist, 80.418

JACQUELINE THURSTON
American   born 1939

196. Untitled (patient receiving radiation treatment), 1979, from the *Medical Series* included in the portfolio *Westcoastnow*, 1979, 10/35, 5⁷⁄₁₆ x 5⁵⁄₁₆" (13.8 x 13.5), Gift of Tamara and Hardy Thomas, 81.180

JERRY N. UELSMANN
American   born 1934

197. *Fleeing Man*, 1961, 7⁵⁄₈ x 8¹⁵⁄₁₆" (18.6 x 22.7), Anonymous gift, 80.333

WEEGEE (Arthur H. Fellig)
American   born Austria
1899-1968

198. *Coffee Break by and with Weegee*, ca. 1940, 7³⁄₈ x 5⁵⁄₁₆" (18.7 x 13.5), Anonymous gift in honor of John Humphrey, 80.338

199. *Bowery Savings Bank (Leg in Stocking)*, 1944, 14 x 11" (35.5 x 27.9), Fund of the 80's Purchase, 84.173

200. *Louella Parsons (Hollywood)*, 1951, 13⁷⁄₁₆ x 10⁵⁄₈" (34.1 x 27.0), Fund of the 80's Purchase, 84.178

201. *M. Monroe*, (distortion made in darkroom from a ca. 1953 negative), ca. 1960, 7½ x 6⁷⁄₈" (19.0 x 17.5), Gift of Graham Nash, 79.417

MINOR WHITE
American   1908-1976

202. Untitled, ca. 1947, 6¹¹⁄₁₆ x 5⁵⁄₈" (17.0 x 14.3), Fund of the 80's Purchase, 84.180

NEAL WHITE
American   born 1947

203. Untitled (two dogs fighting), 1970, from the portfolio, *Meridian/122*, Berkeley, California, 1971, 6³⁄₈ x 9¼" (16.2 x 23.5), Purchase, 71.65.12

204. *San Francisco*, 1978, from the portfolio, *Out of State*, 1978, ed. 29, gelatin silver print with toner, 6⁷⁄₈ x 9⁷⁄₁₆" (17.5 x 24.0), Mrs. Ferdinand C. Smith Fund Purchase, 78.140.4

GARRY WINOGRAND
American   1928-1984

205. *Coney Island—New York City, New York, 1952*, from *Garry Winogrand: A Portfolio of Fifteen Photographs*, 1974, 25/75, 8⁵⁄₈ x 13" (21.9 x 33.0), Gift of Dr. and Mrs. Barry S. Ramer, 83.498

JOEL-PETER WITKIN
American   born 1939

206. Untitled (New Mexico), 1977, gelatin silver print with toner, 8⁷⁄₁₆ x 12⁵⁄₈" (21.4 x 32.1), The Helen Crocker Russell and William H. and Ethel W. Crocker Family Funds Purchase, 80.188

207. Untitled (New Mexico), 1978, gelatin silver print with toner, 8³⁄₈ x 12⁵⁄₈" (21.3 x 32.1), The Helen Crocker Russell and William H. and Ethel W. Crocker Family Funds Purchase, 80.187

208. *Diadaemenos (San Francisco)*, 1981, gelatin silver print with toner, 14¹³⁄₁₆ x 14¼" (37.6 x 36.2), Byron Meyer Fund Purchase, 83.79

209. *Hermes*, 1981, gelatin silver print with toner, 14¹¹⁄₁₆ x 14³⁄₄" (37.3 x 37.5 cm), Gift of Dr. and Mrs. William R. Fielder, 84.210

210. *The Prince Imperial* (New Mexico), 1981, gelatin silver print with toner, 14¹⁵⁄₁₆ x 15" (38.0 x 38.1), Gift of Dr. and Mrs. William R. Fielder, 84.117

The Twentieth-Century Object—
A Perspective from
the Final Decades

VITO ACCONCI
American   born 1940

211. *Bite the Bullet: Slow Guns for Quick Sale (To Be Etched On Your American Mind)*, 1977, photo-etching, 13/25, 28½ x 38³⁄₄" (72.4 x 98.4), Ruth and Moses Lasky Fund and Charles Russell II Fund Purchase, 78.32

THOMAS F. BARROW
American   born 1938

212. *Salt Bird*, 1972, from the series, *Pink Stuff*, gelatin silver print with sepia and gold chloride toners, 4⁷⁄₁₆ x 13½" (11.3 x 34.3), Purchase, 79.256

BERNHARD and HILLA BECHER
German   born 1931
German   born 1934

213. *Silo für Kokskohle, ca. 1920, Kokerei "Eschweiler Reserve," bei Aachen, (Silo for Brown Coal, ca. 1920, Coal Plant "Eschweiler Reserve" near Aachen)*, 1965, 7¹¹⁄₁₆ x 6¹⁄₁₆" (19.5 x 15.4) (A)

Forderturm, ca. 1910, "Blaenserchan" Colliery, Pontypool, Sudwales, (Front Tower, ca. 1910, "Blaenserchan" Colliery, Pontypool, South Wales), 1966, 7⁵⁄₈ x 6¹⁄₁₆" (19.4 x 15.4) (B)

Gasbehalter, ca. 1880, London-Finchley, (Gas Container, ca. 1880, London-Finchley), 1966, 6¹⁄₁₆ x 7¹¹⁄₁₆" (15.4 x 19.5) (C)

Gasbehalter, 1959, Wuppertal (Gas Container, 1959, Wuppertal), 1963, 7¹¹⁄₁₆ x 6¹⁄₁₆" (19.5 x 15.4) (D)

Silo und Mischanlage einer Baustelle, Essen, Ruhrgebiet, (Silo and Mixing Area of a Construction Site, Essen, Ruhr District), 1965, 6¹⁄₁₆ x 7⁵⁄₈" (15.4 x 19.4) (E)

Purchase, 81.185.A-E

214. *Kalköfen, ca. 1920, bei Maubeuge, Nordfrankreich (Lime Kiln, ca. 1920, near Maubeuge, Northern France)*, 1963, 7¹¹⁄₁₆ x 6¹⁄₁₆" (19.5 x 15.4) (F)

Forderturm, 1920, Fosse "Dutemple," Valenciennes, Nordfrankreich (Front Tower, 1920, Fosse "Dutemple," Valenciennes, Northern France), 1967, 7⁵⁄₈ x 6¹⁄₁₆" (19.4 x 15.4) (G)

Kühlturm, ca. 1950, Zeche "Victoria, Mathias," Essen, Ruhrgebiet, (Cooling Tower, ca. 1950, Coal Mine "Victoria, Mathias," Essen, Ruhr District), 1963, 7¹¹⁄₁₆ x 6¹⁄₁₆" (19.5 x 15.4) (H)

Untitled (refinery), ca. 1960–69, 7¹¹⁄₁₆ x 6¹⁄₁₆" (19.5 x 15.4) (I)

Wasserturm, ca. 1920, Liege, Belgien, (Water Tower, ca. 1920, Liege, Belgium), 1968, 7¹¹⁄₁₆ x 6¹⁄₁₆" (19.5 x 15.4) (J)

Purchase, 81.185.F-J

LUIS CARLOS BERNAL
American   born 1941

215. *El Show de Rosita, Barrio Anita*, 1978, from the series, *Espejo: Reflections of the Mexican American*, 1977-78, Ektacolor print, 9¹⁄₁₆ x 9¹⁄₁₆" (23.0 x 23.0), Gift of MALDEF (Mexican American Legal Defense and Educational Fund), 82.165

MICHAEL BISHOP
American   born 1946

216. Untitled (octagonal sign), 1974, Ektacolor print, 10¹⁄₁₆ x 15" (25.6 x 38.1), Gift of Dr. and Mrs. William R. Fielder, 84.202

HARRY BOWERS
American   born 1938

217. *Untitled (HB-24-84)*, 1979/1980, Ektacolor print, 4/10, 49⁷⁄₁₆ x 39¹⁄₂" (125.5 x 100.3), Gift of Dorothy Goldeen, 82.490

STANLEY BOWMAN
American   born 1934

218. *Plastic forks, pot pieces, beet leaves*, 1981, Ektacolor print, 14¹⁄₈ x 18³⁄₁₆" (35.9 x 46.2), Gift of the artist, 82.491

JO ANN CALLIS
American   born 1940

219. *Still Life with Lobster*, 1983, 3/25, 20 x 24" (50.8 x 60.9), Gift of the artist, 83.123

JAMES HAJICEK
American   born 1947

220. Untitled (arrangement of electrical objects), 1979, included in the portfolio, *Westcoastnow*, 1979, 10/35, 14¹⁄₈ x 17¹⁵⁄₁₆" (35.9 x 45.5), Gift of Tamara and Hardy Thomas, 81.159

GYORGY KEPES
American   born Hungary 1906

221. Untitled (dice, crossword puzzle, crystal, paper with raised dots), 1984, Polacolor print, 29¼ x 22" (74.3 x 55.9), Gift of the artist, 85.76

ROBERT PETERS
American   born 1938

222. Untitled (two pears), 1976, from the *School of The Art Institute of Chicago, Graduate Photography Portfolio*, 1976, ed. 75, 9³⁄₄ x 7³⁄₄" (24.8 x 19.7), Purchase, 76.163

DON RODAN
American   born 1950

223. *Art History*, 1977, SX-70 color polaroid print, 3¹⁄₈ x 3¹⁄₈" (7.9 x 7.9), Gift of Henry Krieger, 81.338

224. Untitled (Venus de Milo figurine with artificial asparagus), 1977, SX-70 color polaroid print, 3¹⁄₈ x 3¹⁄₈" (7.9 x 7.9), Gift of Henry Krieger, 81.337

VICTOR SCHRAGER
American   born 1950

225. Untitled, 1978, 7¹¹⁄₁₆ x 9¹¹⁄₁₆" (19.5 x 24.6), Mrs. Ferdinand C. Smith Fund Purchase, 78.180

ROBERT A. WIDDICOMBE
American   born 1949

226. *Cadillac Ranch, Amarillo, Texas*, 1979, Ektacolor print, 13½ x 13½" (34.3 x 34.3), Gift of Dr. and Mrs. William R. Fielder, 84.209

KEVIN WRIGLEY
American   born 1951

227. Untitled (tire sign), ca. 1975, platinum print, 3³⁄₄ x 4³⁄₄" (9.5 x 12.1 cm), Anonymous gift, 80.142